The Change 3

Insights into Self-Empowerment

Jim Lutes ~ Jim Britt

With

Co-authors

The Change 3

Jim Britt ~ Jim Lutes

All Rights Reserved
Copyright 2014

The Change
10556 Combie Road, Suite 6205
Auburn, CA. 95602

The use of any part of this publication reproduced, stored in any retrieval system, or transmitted in any forms or by any means, electronic or otherwise, without the prior written consent of the publisher is an infringement of copyright law.

Jim Lutes ~ Jim Britt

The Change

ISBN: 978-0-692-38602-6

Co-authors

Amanda C. Watts

Naomi Douglas

Julie Anne Christoph

Eden Adele

Sandi Mitchell

George Ishee

Michael E. Schmidlen

Carol Look

Sonja-Sophie

Brian Aubrey Haase

Harry Kroner

Barbara Swanson

Nina Boski

Kurt A. David

Rev. Susan Henley

Glenda Fleming-Thomas

Mark Skovron

Jennifer S. Wilkov

Andy Craig

Marilynn Hughes & Dr. Rudy Schild

The Change is proud to support

Good Women International

Every 5 minutes one American child (many as young as 10 years old) will be abducted and trafficked into the sex trade. 274 children a day. 100,000 each year. And that estimate could be low. The total current number of human trafficking victims in the US alone reaches into the hundreds of thousands and world-wide into the millions.

All profits from the sale of Amazon Kindle electronic books 1 through 4 are being donated to Good Women International, whose focus is on prevention of sexual exploitation of young women and children. They support self-empowerment and educational programs world-wide designed to educate our youth to avoid becoming a victim. A recent successful project was an anti-trafficking curricula for our high schools which is now complete.

Enslavement is a reality. It is documented and it is real. The question is: What are we going to do about it?

To make a donation to Good Women International, a non-profit corporation, go to: www.SupportGoodWomen.com. All donations are tax deductible.

DEDICATION

This book is dedicated to all those seeking change

Foreword

Berny Dohrmann, Chairman of CEO Space International

To The Readers of *The Change* Series

Jim Britt has been a mentor to *Chicken Soup* authors, and to some of the leading thought leaders on earth. Jim Britt's ground breaking work in *Letting Go*, releasing past traumas and betrayals in life to return once again to forward looking manifestation within your full powers, has been instructing at leading *Fortune* companies and to standing room only seminars all over the world. For three decades Jim Britt has been the "trainer of the trainers," of which I am only one. Jim has been an instructor at CEO Space, the most prestigious, hard to get into faculty on the planet, where he developed millions of dollars of resources as he assisted others to develop tens of millions of dollars for their own dream making. Jim is the most "unchanged by success and wealth" man I have ever known. He is an unselfish archangel, like in his book *Rings of Truth*.

Today, Jim Britt and Jim Lutes, along with many inspiring co-authors from around the world, bring a pioneering work to the market to transform your own journey into master manifestation. Their principles are forged on coaching millions on every continent. As you read, you are exploring self-development as the world has yet to practice. In fact, Jim and Jim's publications lead to this one APEX

Foreword

MOMENT. Everything you have done to date in your own life, everyone you have met, every lesson you have learned, has led you to this one GREAT life opportunity... the moment of your own transformation into ever rising full potentials.

As a five time best-selling author myself, as a film maker, and with CEO Space, you can imagine how fussy I am to write a forward to publications in the self-development space. CEO Space was just ranked by *Forbes Magazine* as the leading entrepreneur firm, which hosts five annual business growth conferences serving over 140 countries. It was also named as THE MEETING in the world that YOU CAN NOT AFFORD TO MISS, also by *Forbes*. The world today demands more than a reputation defender to secure your forward brand, it requires that you take responsibility for your own brand and reputation in life. This book will inspire you to do just that.

CEO Space International has supported launches for many amazing works including *Chicken Soup for the Soul, Men Are From Mars, Women Are From Venus, Rich Dad, Poor Dad, The Secret, No Matter What, Three Feet From Gold, Conversations With The King*, and now the movies *Growing Up Graceland* and *Wish Man* (for Make a Wish Foundation), *Outwitting the Devil* by Napoleon Hill and Sharon Lechter, Tony Robbins' great publications, of course Jim Britt's best-selling book *Rings of Truth*, and so many more. The totals have reached more than 2 billion eye balls! You can't play around with that Mount Everest of credibility that I guard like a bank vault!

You can therefore appreciate why I encourage 100% of our followers of all the publications named, to BUY JIM BRITT and JIM LUTES book series *The Change* as a customer recognition for your own ten best close relationships or clients. But don't just buy this book, rather I endorse that you buy 10, and you gift wrap them to acknowledge your most important top ten relationships in life, or clients in business. By doing so you will retain more clients and encourage repeat buying. You may also receive more referrals and strengthen each relationship. The laws of giving will come back to you 10 to 1. When you give freely, you will always receive a rain into your life just as you rain into the lives of those you treasure. Jim Britt, Jim Lutes, and the insightful and inspiring co-authors have given you in *The Change* series, a great opportunity… more important than pouring ice water over someone's head on YouTube as a challenge for charity! The gift that keeps on giving begins when you step up and BUY 10, knowing you have been instrumental in inspiring 10 friends to live a better life. Together we are going to reach 1 BILLION SOULS as we help Jim Britt, Jim Lutes, and their co-authors to achieve their goal to transform human consciousness in our lifetime. Like Zig Ziglar, Jim Rohn, the great Roger Anthony, and so many friends who have passed, my friend Jim Britt is now an historical event in every training, every publication, and every online work at CEO Space. If you ever have the opportunity, STOP YOUR LIFE and see JIM BRITT & JIM LUTES LIVE and you will thank me personally, I know.

Their work is powerful. You'll let go of the baggage you been carrying around for years and learn to embrace everything that creates the future you want and deserve. As you close the pages of any of *The Change* books, you will say over and over again "THANK YOU Jim Britt and Jim Lutes for creating this work." You will gain a new life of super focus as never before and you will commence to master manifest in your own individual life as never before. *The Change* books provide tools to transform results for corporations, institutions and individuals, and once applied it will be impossible to miss your future success in life.

In my opinion, there are only the following areas to embrace for each of us:

Foreword

- Spiritual oneness and balance
- Recreational balance and nature
- Relationship where *Perfection Can Be Had!* (my book)
- Career attainment of goals you, yourself reset along the way
- Parenting either directly or by embracing a child you adopt to mentor at any and every age in life

These perspectives come into alignment within a framework of Jim Britt and Jim Lutes imagination along with decades of human-potential work. My advice is this work is a "BUY 10 TO SHARE WITH FRIENDS" pledge. In fact, a billion readers is a global path that Jim Britt and Jim Lutes are going to achieve NEXT for the world common good.

Let's help in this quest, as both men unselfishly donate their only asset, their precious LIFE TIME, to elevate one life at a time to their full potential and greatness.

My final request to all those who are reading my forward is that you DO IT NOW. When you think of the good you will be doing, just ask yourself, "How long will I make them WAIT?"

I'm buying my 10 today!

Berny Dohrmann

Chairman, CEO Space International

P.S. I so approve this message for all my readers and followers worldwide. CEO Space has helped authors break the book of all records a half a dozen times, which means the only record to beat can be done with the publication you are buying 10 of now. Together we are going to set a global record with one publication. Make the PLEDGE and give the gift of personal development. DO IT TODAY!

Table of Contents

Foreword ix

Jim Britt: How to Win the Competition Against the Clock 1

Jim Lutes: It's Not Where You Are, It's Where You're Going 11

Amanda C. Watts: Awaken Your Magic 21

Andy Craig: Restoration 35

Barbara Swanson: The Change Path 47

Brian Aubrey Haase: What's Causing "NOW" in Your Life? 61

Carol Look, LCSW, EFT Master: Find Your Next Yes 71

Eden Adele: Are You Doing What You Know Or Do You Know What You're Doing? 85

Nina Boski: Rock On With Your Wonderful Bad-Ass Self 97

George Ishee: A Penny for Your Thoughts 109

Jennifer S. Wilkov: Books: A Life-Changing Experience for Reader & Writer Alike 121

Harry Kroner: Deep Healing 133

Julie Anne Christoph, CPC, ELI-MP : Conscious change for a happy life 143

Kurt A. David: My CHANGE 155

Marilynn Hughes & Dr. Rudy Schild: The Science for Moral Law 167

Mark Skovron: The Free Agent Revolution 181

Michael E. Schmidlen: THE Underwear Entrepreneur Asks You: "Who do YOU Listen to???" 197

Naomi Douglas: Facing Divorce and Other Crises: how to allow life to transform you 209

Reverend Susan (Sue) Henley: Just Breathe 219

Sandi Mitchell: Strengthening Your Inner Genius 229

Sonja-Sophie: Food for Thought - Creating a Powerful Mindset 243

Glenda Fleming-Thomas: Contemplating Change 253

AFTERWORD 265

Jim Britt

Jim Britt is an internationally recognized leader in the field of peak performance and personal empowerment training. He is author of 13 best-selling books including, *Cracking the Rich Code, Cracking the Life Code, Rings of Truth, The Power of Letting Go, Freedom, Unleashing Your Authentic Power, Do This. Get Rich-For Entrepreneurs, The Flaw in The Law of Attraction* and *The Law of Realization,* to name a few.

Jim has presented seminars throughout the world sharing his success principles and life enhancing realizations with thousands of audiences, totaling over 1,000,000 people from all walks of life.

Jim has served as a success counselor to over 300 corporations worldwide. He was recently named as one of the world's top 20 success coaches and presented with the best of the best award out of the top 100 contributors of all time to the direct selling industry. He also mentored/coached Anthony Robbins for his first five years in business.

Jim is more than aware of the challenges we all face in making adaptive changes for a sustainable future.

How to Win the Competition against the Clock

By Jim Britt

What's the difference between someone who earns $100,000 a year and someone who earns $1,000,000 a year, other than $900,000? Does he or she work harder? Is the million-dollar earner smarter? Not necessarily intellectually, but certainly with the use of time and energy.

Certainly your life shouldn't be all about making money, even though it is such an integral part of our lives.

The point I want to make is that everyone has about 24 hours a day from which to carve out his or her life. But, if you look at the financial area as an example, what *does* make the difference? It can only be a result of what they do with the time they have… how they "spend" their day.

Accelerated income growth cannot be achieved through incremental steps of doing "more of the same." If you want to move forward quickly, you have to shift into overdrive, into a pattern of new thoughts, beliefs, and actions. Think about it - more of the same can only produce more of the same. Change a little in the right direction and you achieve a little change; change a lot and you get lots of change.

Try harder and you can expect better results, right? Well, possibly to some degree, but not always. Sooner or later you are going to reach a point where you just can't work any harder. There are no more hours in the day and you are stretched to the limit both physically and mentally. You reach a point where your personal output becomes your downfall and trying harder and harder produces less and less. Increased personal efforts can even produce more and bigger problems, like stress, burnout, or anxiety.

I'm not saying that you don't need to have persistence or self-discipline. You need both, and they both can contribute greatly to your success. In fact, it would be hard to have any degree of success without both, because discipline and staying power are essential to producing a successful outcome.

So, if you want more, if you want to move to higher levels of achievement, more effort is not always the answer. What is the answer? How can you make the changes needed to win the competition against the clock? Does it take a miracle to stop the clock long enough to give you a chance to play "catch up?"

Well, I am convinced that everybody can unlock the secrets of maximum personal productivity. I am convinced that everybody can dramatically improve their life, achieve greater financial rewards, and still have more time to enjoy life. I am convinced that everybody can make his or her dreams come true, sooner rather than later.

Two things are essential: the *will* to make a change and the *skill* to become smarter about the use of your time. You can't stop the clock, but you can learn new skills that will allow you to harvest more of what you want in less time. You can become "result oriented" instead of "effort oriented." I'm going to offer you a simple system to follow that, when used daily, will absolutely "turbo charge" your performance. It will show you how to take a broader view of everything you do, to look at your day from a whole different perspective.

How to Win the Competition Against the Clock

Time, as we commonly know it, exists in three forms: past, present, and future. The past is the time we've already spent, the future represents "unused time," and the present is where everything happens. And every second that passes can represent lost opportunity.

Let's look at this in the context of performance. Your past can be an incredible learning resource. Maybe you have discovered something or developed some skill that has worked for you in the past and you can now utilize that same skill to repeat the same actions again. You don't have to relearn the skill all over again. Learning to read is a good example.

In a case where you may have gained less than favorable results, you can use that experience to adjust future actions to avoid repeating the same mistakes again. In both cases, the past can be of great value.

However, none of us can change the result that has already occurred. It's over! We can't push "rewind" and do it over again. It doesn't matter if something happened three years, three months, three hours, or three minutes ago, there is nothing you can do now to change the results you produced in the past, no matter how hard you try. The only value the past has is the knowledge and skills gained from the time you've invested acquiring the experience. Again, it's like learning the skill of driving a car. You don't have to relearn it every time you get behind the wheel. You don't have to get in and say, "Now I wonder how to drive this thing?"

The future, on the other hand, is yet to be determined and is comprised of an unlimited universe of possibilities. Any of these possible futures is where your "someday" dreams, goals, and strategies will be made real, or not. Only time will tell just which possible future will become *your* reality. Time *and* your performance, that is - because when it comes to determining which of the alternative futures actually becomes your reality, it will be your performance right now, in this passing moment, that makes all the difference. There is absolutely nothing you can do, no matter how hard you try, to alter the past; and there is nothing you can do about future results that do not yet exist. What you can do, however, is to make corrections to improve your current actions which will improve your performance and use of time right now.

Becoming more effective with your time is really quite simple - it's realizing that your ability to cause something to occur, from the inception to the completion of a task to the realization of your dreams, can only happen at this moment in time. What you do now can't happen tomorrow. It can only happen now. Look at it this way. If you can perform better right now, the future automatically becomes better. And your actions, performance, aspirations and intention to be a success is what molds the future into what you want.

When you begin to work smarter, you will gain unlimited power over your performance right now, which will deliver to you all your hopes and dreams, sooner rather than later.

Again, there are just twenty-four hours in each day. Do rich people get more than their share? Is there more time allotted to people with certain talents and abilities? We all have the same amount of time - 1,440 minutes each day to spend any way we choose. If you subtract roughly five hundred minutes for sleep, you are left with about nine hundred minutes in which all your dreams will become realized, or they won't.

To get an even clearer picture, try this: divide your day, the nine hundred minutes, into fifteen-minute blocks of time. That's sixty blocks. Your fifteen-minute blocks of time begin ticking away the second you jump out of bed in the morning. If you hit the fifteen-minute snooze alarm, there goes one block, and you now have fifty-nine left. You spend a half hour reading the newspaper, there goes two more 15 minute blocks. You work out for 30 minutes, there goes another two blocks of time. You spend one fifteen-minute block after another, from the beginning to the end of your day. The question is, how are you spending them?

In my first experiment with counting time, I decided to track where I spent my time for an entire month. If you want an awakening, try doing this. Every fifteen minutes, write down what you did for the last fifteen-minute block of time. Shower, shave, and get dressed, three blocks. Eat breakfast, thirty minutes, two blocks of time spent. Drive to the office, thirty minutes, another couple of fifteen-minute blocks. Watch television for two hours, that's eight blocks spent.

I remember having a two-hour business lunch that was completely nonproductive. As I wrote it down on my calendar eight fifteen-minute blocks, it was a rude awakening. I suddenly got a totally different view of my day and why I had a problem getting all the things done that I wanted to do. Once you become aware that the fifteen-minute blocks are ticking away day after day, the question becomes, what are you going to do with each block?

This is a very different view of your day from the traditional time planners and appointment schedules. What you have here is a countdown that starts when you get up in the morning and runs out when you go to bed about sixty blocks of time later. And there is nothing you or anyone else can do to gain back even one minute from your countdown clock. When your 900 minutes are over, they're over. When each fifteen-minute block is over, it's over. The question is, "What did you do with your last one?" And, more importantly, what are you going to do with your next one? Learn from your last fifteen-minute block. And if you stop to regret how you spent your last block, wishing you'd done it differently, you are only wasting the next block of time. So, don't spend *any* time regretting mistakes, move on! It's over! Next!

When you begin to break down your day into "bite-sized" portions, you become aware of your performance in the present, right now, which is all you have anyway. I call these fifteen-minute bite-sized portions "power points." When you look at your day in this way, you no longer lose hours of time and wonder where it went. You now have sixty chances to put forth your best efforts and to gain more rewards sooner! You also have sixty chances, sixty power points, to make corrections to your actions and improve your performance. You are now in total control of the present moment, where the real action is taking place. And if you find yourself off track, you can quickly move in the right direction toward your desired outcome. Plan for the future, yes, but stay focused on the present moment where the action takes place.

Try this exercise for the next week or so, and watch how your performance immediately improves. Every fifteen minutes, stop for a moment and ask yourself, "Did my actions during the last fifteen minutes move me closer to my desired results, and if not, why not?" If not, what can you do differently in the next fifteen minutes that will move you in the right direction faster?

People say that they don't have enough time, but if you stop, really stop, and consider how you are spending your time you'll find your production increasing, more time to relax and enjoy life, less stress, and so much more.

The reality is that no one can perform at their optimum level and achieve the success they want without first doing something about their fifteen-minute blocks of time. Fifteen minutes is the perfect slot of time, because it's enough time for you to do something significant toward what you want to accomplish. And it's short enough that if you find yourself moving away from your objective, you can correct your actions before you waste a lot of time going the wrong way. There's nothing worse, in my thinking, than discovering at the end of your day that you have been moving really fast in the wrong direction and you've wasted sixty fifteen-minute blocks of time. We all do it, and in this busy world it is easy to do without realizing that it is even happening.

A good example is to just watch yourself as you waste time scrolling through social media or surfing the internet. I'm not talking about productive time you spend doing these things if it contributes to the success of your business. I'm talking about "busyness" trying to fill your time to keep from doing something more productive. In other words, looking for the real reason you may be wasting your time. Is it avoiding reality, avoiding a fear of failure, etc.

Gaining just fifteen minutes each day can be very powerful. In fact, over the course of a year, you would gain an extra ninety-one hours. That's over two working weeks! What if you improved eight of your 15 minute blocks a day? That's two hours a day you might gain in productivity. What about all sixty? What if you saved yourself an hour in each workday? That's more than eight 40-hour work weeks in a year. What could you do with those extra weeks each year - get rich, enjoy life more, take an extended vacation, produce more?

When you become more observant of your actions, the time you spend on them, and the results you are actually producing, only then will you be able to improve your performance at will.

This method of increasing your performance means that you will never again take for granted any fifteen-minute block of time. Observe yourself periodically throughout the day and ask yourself, "Right now, am I producing the results that I'm capable of getting with the time I'm investing?" And after you apply this method of self-observation for a while, it will become second nature, a habit.

To find out more about Jim's work:

www.JimBritt.com

http://PowerOfLettingGo.com

http://CrackingTheRichCode.com

http://FaceBook.com/JimBrittOnline

http://JourneyBeginsNow.com

Jim Lutes

Having taught his branded form of human performance since the early 1990s, Mr. Lutes has accelerated top level entrepreneurs throughout his career by conducting trainings on personal growth and subconscious programming into worldwide markets.

During this time Jim took his skills regarding the human mind, and combining it with trainings on influence, persuasion and communication strategies, he launched Lutes International in the early 1990s. Based in San Diego California, Jim has taught seminars for corporations, sales forces, individuals and athletes. Having appeared on television, radio and worldwide stages, Jim's style, knowledge and effectiveness provide profound results.

"Jim Lutes possesses a unique ability to create performance change in an individual in a fraction of the time it takes his competitors." The core of humans decisions are based on the programs we acquire, reinforce and grow. Combining Jim's various trainings, individuals can reach new levels of achievement and fulfillment in all areas of life. The results are at times nothing short of astonishing.

"My goal is to take that embryonic greatness that exists inside every person in America, foster it, empower it, and then hand them personal strategies based on solid principles that allow them to take that new attitude and apply it to creating a life by design."

It's Not Where You Are, It's Where You're Going

By Jim Lutes

Who are you right now? Do you know how much power you actually have to create the life you dream of? Can you say that in every moment of the day you are consciously aware of your decisions and habits, and that they all serve your highest interests? Are all the elements of your life aligned? By this I mean, finances, relationships, health and emotional well-being. If anyone of these is off, all of them are off. Is anything off in your life right now? If something is off, do you know what you need to do to re-align so that everything in your life flows harmoniously and with ease?

The concept that we are the creators of our own lives is not new, however it is not widely believed by everyone, and it's certainly not taught in schools! Have you ever felt like you were the victim of circumstances outside of your control? We all have. What we so often fail to realize is that even in those circumstances, indeed in any circumstances, we still have choice. We are still playing an active role in the outcome of our situation. Our choices, however, are often born out of the result of our previous life experiences and how they have affected us. More commonly than not, we make choices and decisions, to the tune of several each day, without even consciously thinking about them. When I ask people about their belief systems and the habits and patterns that basically control their lives, I am often struck by how few of these beliefs and habits were ever chosen by that person on a conscious level. In other words, the rules that are guiding your life about how to live your own life are very often picked up unconsciously. If you want to create a life that is a masterpiece, it is essential that you begin to reprogram your mind.

You are the creator of your life. Your thoughts - and particularly the visual element of what you are thinking - serve to create your day-to-day experience. Do you want a life that is a stick figure drawing, or a plain old paint-by-numbers creation? Or are you yearning to create a vibrant masterpiece of a life, filled with all of the dreams you long for?

When you were a child, your identity formed and for most of us, this identity was formed out of the stories about ourselves that our families or other significant people told us, or experiences, or even our own decisions made to help get our needs met and survive our childhoods. I believe identity is the strongest force in the human personality. Believe it or not, what shapes you the most is not your capability, but your identity. When I say identity, I mean the rules you have created to support who you *think* you are. The problem is that most of us defined ourselves a long time ago. If we defined our identity a long time ago, and we start to see it doesn't really fit who we have grown into, when we step outside that definition, we become really uncomfortable. There is a strong pull in the human personality to remain consistent, and thanks to this pull, we long to remain consistent with how we define ourselves. One of the deepest human needs we have is for certainty, and if this is the case, and we do not know who we are, then we do not know how to act. We start to define ourselves early on, and tell ourselves stories to go along with the definition, stories like "I'm ugly" or "I'm a loser" or "I can't catch a break" and others. We don't always recognize when we have grown out of these stories, and instead let them linger on. We stay in an outdated identity because we love consistency and certainty. However, we don't have to get caught up in these stories and have them taint our masterpieces any longer. We can reprogram our minds and step out of limiting beliefs, re-creating our identities to match who we have evolved to become in our lives.

Before we get into re-programming our minds, however, let's go back to the beginning. How did limiting thoughts and beliefs even get into our minds? How did our identity become defined?

Without going into too much detail, I want to explain in a simple way, the different levels the brain functions on. Our brains operate on four different wavelengths – alpha, beta, theta and delta. The alpha level is the level we pass through to go to sleep and to wake up again, and is the most common level the brain is in when one is in a trance state. Most of the time, when we are awake, the adult brain operates at the beta level. This is when our eyes are focused, our conscious mind is in control, and we are thinking in a logical way. The theta level is in action during states of deeper trance, or dreaming. The delta level is in operation during deep sleep.

When we are in the alpha level, we are highly receptive. The messages we take in while in this level go straight to our subconscious mind. One major difference between the brains of children and adults is that a child's brain operates primarily at the alpha level. This explains why children are so impressionable. Our parents, and other significant people from our childhood had a tremendous impact on the messages that our subconscious mind received. Events from our childhood had a strong impact on our self-image, our identity and how we developed as adults. To take this back to identity, hopefully now the picture is becoming more clear that you may or may not have had as much control over your identity as you believe you do now. What you absorbed as a child had a profound impact on your identity, not to mention on choices and decisions you continue to make in your adult life today.

Another way to look at this is to think of your mind as a nightclub. When you were a child, there was a bouncer at the door who let everyone in. You did not have a filter yet - in this case, a bouncer who was discerning. So everyone came in – negative thoughts, negative memories, positive thoughts, lessons learned, experiences both positive and negative. Everyone and everything got into your nightclub from the moment you were born. Now imagine that as you grow older, the bouncer decides he is going to start to be more discerning about who is already in your nightclub. You might try to allow a new positive, affirming thought into your nightclub, only there is a nightclub full of negative memories, beliefs and other thoughts that are crowding out the positive thoughts you are trying to re-populate your nightclub with.

This is why we find ourselves in a position where we live life a particular way. We believe we were raised in a particular way, and we act in a particular way. Throughout our lives, in an effort to avoid pain and continue to meet our needs, we made critical decisions about who we are and how we thought we needed to be. We believe we know who we are, but the way we have behaved for years is simply an adaptation. It was just something that happened as we were trying get our basic needs met, as we were trying to get the love, respect or acceptance from a parent, sibling, peer, lover or other loved one. This caused us to make key decisions that enabled us to adapt to the circumstances around us. We may not realize for years that we have become experts at living in our identities, despite the fact that these identities do not reflect our true nature, rather the conditioning and other influences we were raised with. So many ideas and beliefs that were never even ours passed into our minds from the moment we were born, and so many of these served to help us get our needs met through childhood and adolescence. So many of these ideas and beliefs have become more and more obsolete as we move through adulthood. Even if you feel like you held your own when you were growing up, and that the relationships you had as a child, especially with your mother and father, were strong, and you feel like you are strong as a result, there are still patterns your subconscious mind is running that no longer serve you. It is the experience of having to deal with all of the events of your past - and this includes events that may have happened before you were born, in your parents' past - all of these events affect your decision making, your relationships, your finances, your choices, behaviors and life circumstances, even today.

In order to move into the fullness of our potential, we have to be able to clear out the beliefs and thoughts that are negative and are no longer needed. After all, it is not what you accomplish in relation to others that is important, it's what you accomplish in relationship to your own potential. Your tomorrow is based on your today, and once you realize that the ability to create your brightest tomorrow is already within you, you will start moving in the best direction for yourself, the direction of change for the better.

This is the basis of the work I am inviting you to do with this book. As you create your life masterpiece, you will have to kick some of those dancers out of the nightclub. If you don't make space in the nightclub for some positive thoughts or new thoughts, those thoughts won't stay because it's full of negative thoughts. So you need to empty the whole nightclub, evict the negative thoughts and limiting beliefs, and start to only let the positive and affirming thoughts in. The bouncer needs to wake up and actively guard the nightclub to only allow in those thoughts and beliefs that serve you. We go along in life and we often don't even want to see the occupants of our nightclub, sometimes even self-medicating so we can stay in denial. Somehow a lot of the negative thoughts and beliefs that got into the nightclub serve us and have served us through the years, helping us to survive. But that doesn't mean they need to stay!

The Change 3

It is incredible how common it is when people begin to reassess their lives and their relationships, with themselves and others, or the success they are having (or perhaps not having), they discover that much of what has been negatively affecting their lives, their achievements, their finances, their careers, their intimate relationships, and even their bodies, was influenced by their parents. Not necessarily by the problems of their parents, but by trying to be liked, approved of, or appreciated by one or both parents. In many cases, the decisions people have made from childhood on were about avoiding the pain that was inflicted on them by a parent or loved one. So we can be forty, fifty, even eighty years old, and we are still living the strategies we lived as children. What's worse is that as we grew up we often told ourselves "I'll never be like that!" Yet here you are today, quite possibly exactly like that. You don't want to admit it, but if you watched a film of your interactions, you might say "Oh dear, I never wanted to be like that parent," yet you are. Or, if you didn't become the parent you said you would never become, you may have gone in the entirely opposite direction, and you are not like that parent at all, but now you are something else. You are the opposite of the extreme you didn't like. Now you are another extreme, but that doesn't work either. No one teaches us this, so it becomes unconscious and we don't even see it. It stays within us and remains part of the invisible fabric of our thinking and our decision-making every single day.

Where you are in your life right now is the direct result of making decisions unconsciously, stuck in patterns and beliefs that served you once, but have not evolved to continue to serve you now, as an adult. If you feel stuck or are not pleased with your circumstances, being aware of the choices you make – choices that come from someplace other than your conscious thoughts - is step number one to getting out of the paint-by-numbers life and into the masterpiece. If you feel great about your life, you can also benefit from this work, as there are still countless limiting beliefs and thoughts in your subconscious mind that affect you too, whether you realize it or not.

It's not about where you are, it's about where you're going. If you want to change your life and align all major aspects of your life – finances, health, relationships, emotional well-being – then looking at what shaped you and stepping out of a limiting identity is what will help you to make the changes you seek.

It's amazing to me how people take more time in a day to pick out what they are going to watch on TV than on programming their minds. We spend more time choosing what kind of products we're going to use to clean our bodies than how we are going to clean our minds! We put so much emphasis on the external, when it is the internal that determines the external. If you want success in money, relationships, health and emotional health you must start to work from the inside out.

It all comes down to the power of your mind, and this includes both your conscious and subconscious mind. You have in your power the ability to transform your thoughts into your allies or your adversaries. You are manifesting your life based on your thoughts. The universe, or source, or whatever higher power there is for you, responds to images that come to your mind. You have in your life exactly what you tell yourself you want; that is, if you are frustrated, you're telling yourself you're frustrated. If you're saying, "I'm sick," then you are not enjoying good health. Our internal communication is the dialogue we have with ourselves each day, and it is mostly filled with old programming. I like to do an exercise at my seminars where I ask a participant to repeat "I have a fatal disease" twenty times. As you may imagine, no one ever agrees to do this. Why not? Because they are afraid of making it manifest for themselves. Yet those same participants go home after the seminar and tell themselves they're broke, they can't pay the bills, they're unlovable, any manner of negative and diminishing thoughts, without even recognizing what they are doing! This is how our subconscious minds work, without our even being aware of how they are working behind the scenes to sabotage us. Our internal communication perpetuates that realization of what we expect.

If your internal communication is laden with limiting beliefs, or running on patterns that have been held in your subconscious for your whole life, then you will not be able to create your life masterpiece. Your patterns of thought and beliefs that no longer serve you must be sacrificed if you want to align all elements of your life and step into your masterpiece. When I say "It's not where you are, it's where you're going," this is what I'm talking about. Where you are right now, as you read this, continues to be the self that is held hostage by an identity formed when you were a child. You are being held hostage by the patterns your subconscious is running in the background of your every waking moment. Until you re-program your mind and make conscious choices in place of these choices of habit, you will not be able to move yourself out of where you might feel stuck and into where you will prosper. I'm not talking about prosper financially either! I'm talking about prospering in whatever area wants to prosper – health, relationships, emotional well-being, sure - finances too. The big picture "prosper" - another word for it is thrive. To move from surviving to thriving means moving forward into where you're going, and not staying settled into where you are.

Take stock of where you are right now, and see if you can bridge the gap between where you are, and where you want to go. Where you are going in your life depends upon the choices you make today. Picking up this book was one choice you made that might serve you as you create your masterpiece. Eating a donut mindlessly on your drive home from work was one choice that may have been completely unconscious, one that may have served your eight-year-old self, starving for love from your mother, but one that doesn't serve your vision of being fit and strong. Pay attention to the choices you make today – these will directly affect your tomorrow.

This is a unique opportunity to look deep inside yourself. Take a good look inside of your relationships, your decisions about money, and your decisions about your career, your relationship with the universe, or your higher power, and even your body. Start to understand how your own upbringing has influenced you and start spotting some of the decisions you have made, including pinpointing one core decision that has affected your identity. Get clear about what really stands in your way (hint: it's you!) to creating your very own life masterpiece.

To contact Jim:

info@lutesinternational.com

www.lutesinternational.com

www.jimluteslive.com

Amanda C. Watts

Amanda C. Watts takes talented coaches who are struggling to have the audience and income they deserve, and helps them have clarity on their purpose in life, align it with their passions and create a life they love, doing what they love!

Amanda is a successful entrepreneur, author, speaker, and is known as The Coaches 'Coach'.

Amanda started her entrepreneurial journey in 2009, and spent many years trying to make her business grow. It was only when she uncovered the best-kept entrepreneurial secret (clarity on passion and purpose) and changed her mindset that her business and life flourished.

By aligning her purpose in life with her passions, she helps women around the world awaken their magic and have amazing lives that they only dreamed of. With Amanda's mentoring, these women then master how to share their authentic gifts with the world and make it a better place.

Amanda has presented seminars and talks sharing her success principles of marketing and mindset, and in 2014 she set up the Clients In Abundance Business Academy with her husband. The Clients In Abundance Business Academy shows coaches how to have successful businesses using the 5 Essential Business Pillars For Success.

Amanda lives with her husband and two children, in the South of England.

Awaken Your Magic

By Amanda C Watts

As I write this chapter I am a little under a month from turning 40. I have lived many lives during my years… I have played the part of granddaughter, daughter, mother, wife, friend, employee, and entrepreneur…

I have been fortunate enough to travel the world far and wide, and have earned a healthy living working for someone else, and an even healthier living working for myself.

But for me, my magical journey really started in 2010 when one man, Stephen, and a two-hour meeting, changed my life forever. And what I share with you today could change your life forever, too.

Less than six months prior to this meeting and life-changing moment, my two children (aged 5 and 8) and I, were homeless and penniless, having just escaped a highly toxic relationship.

I was in this situation because of a series of bad decisions and events.

So let my story begin:

I had known Stephen for moments prior to the meeting (I was hoping he would hire me to write his newsletters) and after the event I was never to see him again.

I didn't know it at the time, but the Universe's purpose for this meeting was for me to receive this piece of information, and nothing more.

What I am about to explain to you is how one small piece of information can change your life… if you ACT on it.

How one shift in your mindset and your outlook on life can change your destiny, your dreams and awaken the magic within you.

What Stephen and I discussed meant I went from nothing to Abundance, in a very short space of time:

My new business became aligned with my passion and my purpose, my children were happier, I returned to my roots just outside of London, and I met my now, husband. In 2014, we got married and he is the most amazing life partner, business partner and stepfather to my two beautiful children.

I now run a highly profitable business I love, helping people just like you create a life you love, living your purpose and with passion.

This is how I did it, take heed and you can too:

Awaken Your Magic™

Would you like to:

- Wake up every day knowing you were doing what you were put on this earth to do?

- Live joyfully in the home of your dreams?

- Enjoy fulfilling relationships with people who you love to spend time with?

- Excel in your chosen livelihood?

- Earn money easily and without fear?

- Be passionate and excited about your future?

- Wake up every day grateful, and genuinely happy to be alive?

- Be able to manifest anything you can dream of?

All of this, and more, is achievable for everyone, no matter your background, your wealth or your current or past situations.

A Great Law

So what was it that Stephen told me that day in his office? He told me to watch a film, about a secret that has been passed down through the ages about a great and powerful law.

This powerful law was brought into the commercial world by Rhonda Byrne in the 2006 movie The Secret (which is currently available to watch for free on YouTube; I suggest if you have never watched it then you must). This Law is called the Law of Attraction.

The Law of Attraction

The Law of Attraction has been described as the doorway; the key to unlocking life's full potential and the essence that animates the whole Universe. It can exist and work for anyone, including you.

In essence it works around the principles:

    'Thoughts Become Things'

        and

    'Like Attracts Like'

In basic terms the Law of Attraction is:

What you think about today determines your reality tomorrow.

What you concentrate your thoughts on becomes your reality. Worry attracts more worry. Anxiety attracts more anxiety. Unhappiness attracts more unhappiness.

The opposite is also true.

Happiness attracts more happiness, gratitude attracts more gratitude. Kindness attracts more kindness and love attracts more love.

It is imperative that you see inside of you, and keep yourself in check at all times.

When I was barely scraping a living a few years ago, and felt desperate for a 'lucky break,' Stephen told me of the Law of Attraction, and I learned that to change my world all I needed to do was to change the way I felt inside.

How easy is that?

At the time, I knew nothing of the Universe and how it guides and communicates with us in every second of our lives. I didn't know how it responded to my thoughts.

I didn't realize that spending three days in bed feeling sorry for myself was exasperating the problem. My feelings of sorrow grew worse every day - because I was focusing on feeling sad, I was attracting more sadness. It was getting worse and worse.

But after watching The Secret and learning about The Law of Attraction, I knew to look for the gifts in everything, especially when facing a negative situation.

There is much to glean from every incident and happening. You must look for the positive in everything, because everything we attract causes us to grow, this means that everything is for our own good.

I now know that a broken marriage, a toxic relationship and being homeless were lessons, positive lessons. I now know that my children being unhappy and me having to be a better mum to overcome this, was a positive lesson. I now know that having nothing is a positive lesson, one that led to me having everything.

Adjusting to a new path, and new directions enabled me to gain new qualities and strengths, and have brought me to the Abundance I have today, for which I am so very grateful.

Think of the wealthiest people in the world. They have been able to attract everything in the world they want because they have thought about their deepest desires, and acted on it…

Imagine if you really knew what was inside of you, what really made your heart sing and why you were put on this earth.

If you knew this, do you think you would be able to Awaken Your Magic™ and manifest all your desires? Because the combination of passion and purpose will enable you to utilize the Law of Attraction fully.

The Law of Attraction works if you erase negativity in your life; negative thoughts, actions and feelings, and embrace positivity.

And the Law of Attraction works even if you have hit rock bottom in life. I know as I am living proof, as are so many other happy and wealthy people.

You see, if you know how to manifest what you really want in life then this gives you a HUGE advantage over others. If you think nothing but negative thoughts in life, than that is what you will manifest, the worst things in life will come to you, because that is what you are attracting.

However, if you are positive and focus on the good things, and what you want to manifest, that will be attracted to you.

So whenever you feel down, force your mind to discard the negative thoughts. Dwell on affirmative thoughts and slowly embrace positive emotions as well.

No matter where you are, no matter how difficult things might appear, you are being moved towards Abundance, always.

Do this, and within days or weeks you *will see* a noticeable improvement in your life.

Passion and Purpose

Of course the true magnificence of the Law of Attraction shows itself when you awaken the magic within you.

You see inside each and every one of you is a gift that you have to share with the world and a passion for something that makes your heart sing.

Unless you are living a life you love, doing what you love, it's virtually impossible to turn it into a successful and profitable life, business or career…

An example of this is when I set up a copywriting business back at the start of 2010. I was writing copy for local businesses in Wiltshire: newsletters, websites, etc., and at the same time I was giving away marketing advice for free… and it was the marketing advice that was making such a huge difference to my clients, not the copy I was writing for £25 an hour.

To top it off, I hated doing the copywriting, but thought because it was a tangible 'thing' it would be easy to charge for… I was wrong.

Let me use the example of 'stuffing' and 'turkey' to explain:

I was charging for the stuffing (copywriting) but the juicy turkey (marketing expertise) was handed to them on a plate! And do you know why? I found it so natural to speak about and teach marketing, that I didn't place a value on it.

I read about marketing every day, spoke about it to everyone and dreamt about it at night. I became the go-to expert in Wiltshire for marketing advice… yet I never charged a penny, but the value I gave was huge!

It was only when I got myself a business coach that it became clear that I had to stop copywriting. My passion was marketing, and my purpose in life was to help others with this.

I was put on this earth to help people get clear on what they provided and create a business that THEY loved, aligned with their purpose in life. Then, and only then, could they create a successful business that lead to profits.

It wasn't about the stuffing (copywriting), but about the turkey (passion, purpose, profits).

I needed a coach to help get this truth out of me. We all need a coach at points in our lives, whether it's a health, life or business coach.

Your Passion and Your Purpose

Awakening Your Magic and knowing your passion and purpose with clarity will enable you to consciously evoke the Law of Attraction.

Ask yourself these questions to help you get passion and purpose clarity:

- What could you do all day for free that is of huge value to people?

- What makes you jump out of bed in the morning?

- What books are on your nightstand?

- What would you do if you knew you could not fail?

- What topic or subject are you the go-to person for? (Remember everyone came to me for marketing advice, even though I was marketing myself as a copywriter.)

- What gives you happiness and excitement in your life?

- What do you think you could be among the best in the world at doing?

- If you had to choose one thing that you'd do for free for the rest of your life, what would it be?

Questions control your focus. What you focus on is what you will manifest; remember the Law of Attraction and "thoughts become things."

Ask yourself empowering questions and you will find empowering answers... Live a life you love, with passion and on purpose... Awaken Your Magic™.

Take Consistent Action

Persist, persist, persist. You see, consistency is key and persistence is imperative for the principles to become second nature for you. You also have to be specific and set goals.

- If you want a successful business, you can't just set up a website and hope it will bring you clients.

- If you want the house of your dreams, you can't just wish to win the lottery and hope it will come to you.

- If you want to lose 40 pounds and get fit, you can't just sit eating donuts and crisps all day whilst watching TV.

You have to know what you want, what you need to do to achieve it, plan what you need to do, and act on it. Consistently.

You may have heard the saying: "If you chase two rabbits you will catch neither." Well this is what I want you to think about when you focus on creating the life you want to live, doing what you love.

You have to decide on the ONE thing you want to achieve, and then subsequently, each ONE action that is going to get you to achieve the one thing you wish to achieve.

It is about being focused and consistent…

And you also have to be really specific in the one thing.

For me, I wish to coach 2,000 women in the next five years; and enable them to awaken their magic by aligning their passion and purpose so they can create a highly profitable business, whilst making a positive difference to the world.

Get a piece of paper and a pen and let me show you what I mean:

The Change 3

When you Awaken Your Magic™ and you know how to align your passion and your purpose, what will success look like to you?

Write down how you want your life and business to look in 5 years' time?

Now we are going to work backwards and create the ONE action you need to do to achieve this success…

Write down answers to the following:

- What is the ONE action you need to complete in 3 years for the 5 year success?

- What is the ONE action you need to complete in 1 year to complete the 3 year task?

- What is the ONE action you need to complete in 6 months to complete the 1 year task?

- What is the ONE action you need to complete in 1 month to complete the 6 month task?

- What is the ONE action you need to complete in 1 week to complete the 1 month task?

- What is the ONE action you need to do today to complete the weekly task?

- What is the ONE action you need to do now, to complete today's task, and set you on the path to your 5-year success?

If you look at your paper you will see a list of actions to get you to your goal. The focus you have on one action, and one action alone, will enable you to easily leverage the Law of Attraction. You will be able to turn your thoughts into success, as you will have focus and action covered!

The Right Attitude

Your success in life is also about having the right attitude, and how grateful you are for what you attract every day.

7 years ago, life was very different for me. Every day was a burden, I didn't eat and I didn't enjoy life. I was in an awful toxic relationship that left my children and me exhausted, unhappy and disheartened with the world.

It was only when I realized I had a choice to get out of this situation, change my life for the better, adopt a 'can-do' attitude, that I saw the power of attitude and gratitude.

We all have the potential to achieve great things in life. Our attitude is the deciding factor in our success…

When I began practicing the Law of Attraction, invested in coaching and personal development, and stayed positive - my health, wealth and happiness was abundant.

I met the man of my dreams, my children were happier and my business became a six-figure success in less than seven months (I had struggled to earn more than £1000 a month for many years prior).

Practicing The Art Of Gratitude

We 'like' posts on Facebook and 'favorite' tweets on Twitter, but being thankful every day for the small things in our lives is something that so many people fail to do.

We are all on a healing journey of some sort, whether it is from illness, emotional blows or loss of loved ones.

We all WANT our lives to be more fulfilled, richer, more connected with the world around us, yet often fail to see the good in what surrounds us.

The problem is we get mired in fear, negativity and despair. And we all too often have a bad habit and sweat the small stuff. But not anymore!

Gratitude is one of the most powerful emotions you can use to bring absolute abundance. Gratitude dispels negativity, no matter what form it has taken.

The art of gratitude is a powerful practice to ground yourself in the present moment and invites a feeling of thankfulness for everything and everyone that is in your life right now.

How to Practice the Art of Gratitude:

1. Before you write anything, say 'thank you' three times.
2. List three things you are grateful for in the present tense. For example: 'I am truly grateful that money comes easily and flows towards me.'
3. Always start your sentence with: 'I am truly grateful' 'I am so grateful now' or 'thank you.' Keep it positive.
4. Make writing at least three things you are grateful for a daily habit.

I cannot describe the unfathomable power you are summoning through the Universe when you master practicing the art of gratitude.

Magic and Abundance

My life changed when I learned about the Law of Attraction. It changed further when I aligned my passion and life's purpose and created a business and life I love! It is now your turn to Awaken Your Magic™.

A final thought:

What you hold in your mind will tend to be what occurs in your life.

If you continue to believe what you have always believed, you will continue to act in the way you have always acted.

If you continue to act in the way you have always acted, you will continue to get what you have always got.

Know thyself and change your thoughts, actions and attitude and be grateful…

Awaken Your Magic™ and have abundant success…

With much love and gratitude,

Amanda C Watts

To contact Amanda

www.awakenyourmagic.com

www.clientsinabundance.com

amanda@clientsinabundance.com

Andy Craig

Since the country's change in leadership in 2008, Andy Craig has been challenged by the gradual breakdown in our nation's governing core values. He's watched as our government has replaced fiscal responsibility with unbridled spending, strong leadership with amoral posturing, and hard work with entitlement. He's witnessed first-hand the "change" the current administration has promised, but that change hasn't been for the better.

Andy Craig is an entrepreneur and army veteran willing to fearlessly compete with career politicians to affect a change for our nation. Andy ran for the United States Senate in Oklahoma with the desire to help restore strength of character to a government system screaming for solid leadership. He isn't interested in playing politics, he's interested in affecting change.

Andy's business experience in client services has taught him to listen to people and then work to find a solution. He has honed the negotiation skills necessary to get things done and holds a Bachelor of Arts in Speech in the Business Environment. Andy is also a member of Toastmasters International, which has given him the persuasive skills and confidence necessary to move forward on the current issues that are valued most important to Americans.

Andy and his wife, Michelle, live in Broken Arrow, Oklahoma. They are small business owners, have strong moral values, and an excellent work ethic. They are also both passionate about helping people live healthier, happier lives.

Restoration

By Andy Craig

Change. Change is something everyone searches for. The question is, what kind of a change are you seeking? Are you seeking a change in a relationship, career, or financial situation? For some of us, it is not so much *change* that we seek, but rather *restoration*. In many cases, we already know what needs to be done, we just simply have not done it. It is *restoration* to what we once knew, and to the roots that were sown long ago. No matter what area you are seeking, change or restoration, there are consistent steps that are needed to achieve this.

Every change we seek has certain elements within it. First and foremost, we must know what change is necessary and how to measure the results of this change. The easiest way to measure our results is by having a goal; the magnitude of the change that you seek, will determine the size of the goal.

How big of a goal are you setting for yourself? When I look at goal setting, I like to use an acronym which I am sure some of you may be familiar with. That acronym is BHAG. It stands for Big Hairy Audacious Goal. This kind of a goal or dream is one that is so big, so huge, you barely believe that you can achieve it.

In this chapter, I am sharing with you an experience that I recently had in seeking change.

My name is Andy Craig. I recently experienced setting my own big hairy audacious goal. I ran for United States Senate in the June 24, 2014 primary in the state of Oklahoma. This was a huge goal which is still in process for me, because I did not accomplish this the first time around. However, I learned a great deal from setting this goal and going after it. The truth is, success is the progressive realization of a worthy goal and I learned a ton from this experience.

What is your BHAG?

Once you decide what your BHAG is, determine why it is that you are going after this goal. Your "why" is your key to achieving your goal, it is your fuel for achieving your goal. Without knowing your "why," your goal has a much lower chance of being realized and achieved. To achieve your goal, you will encounter many obstacles and challenges and your "why" is what will carry you through these challenges.

So once you have determined your BHAG, become clear on why you are achieving this. Your reason must be crystal clear to you and should evoke emotion from within you. Emotion is what moves you through the challenge that you are facing as you achieve your goal. Logic does not move you through your challenge, emotion moves you through your challenge.

For example, let's say a child is trapped under a car and the child's mother is trying to save her child's life. Under normal circumstances, the mother would not be able to lift this car, however, with her child's life in danger, she is able to muster up super-human strength to lift this car and save her child's life. This is an emotional "why."

I had a desire to run for the United States Senate, which I believe came from the Lord. Because of this, I prayed about this and asked the Lord why he wanted me to run; He told me that this nation had strayed from the principles on which it was founded and people were seeking someone that would be true to the founding principles. I found this to be true as one of the main ideals that I learned during my campaign, that people are ready for a change. However, it's not like the change that we have seen since 2008. The people that I spoke with and that I heard comments from shared with me they are ready for, what I would consider, a restoration. People in this nation are ready for a restoration to where this nation has come from.

My campaign platform represented the restoration of the traditional values on which this nation was founded. Let me give you a visual for what I mean.

I compared our nation and our value system to a fruit tree. When a fruit tree is healthy it produces big, juicy, succulent fruit that we desire to eat and truly enjoy. However, when a fruit tree has a diseased root system, it produces shriveled, nasty, ugly fruit that we have no desire to eat. Our nation is like a fruit tree with a diseased root system. Our nation's leadership core values are producing some very poor fruit - such as: $18 trillion in debt and counting, a question as to what is life, a question as to what is marriage, and a question as to what should we as Americans should be allowed to do with respect to our religious expression.

Our core values must be restored to what our founding fathers had in mind when they founded our nation. Once these core values have been restored, our root system will be restored, and our nation will begin producing healthy fruit again. It will take time for our fruit to be restored once our root system is restored, but it will happen.

Now that you understand what my "why" was, what is your "why?" Why must you achieve your goal or your dream? What is your reason for accomplishing this goal?

The next step in achieving your big goal is to visualize or see yourself already accomplishing your goal. I did this by seeing myself speaking in front of audiences and captivating their attention. I saw myself meeting every person in the room and introducing myself to them. Lastly, I saw myself winning the election with 50.1% of the vote or more. Athletes do this all the time. In basketball, athletes visualize themselves making their baskets, especially with free throws. I have heard studies comparing the results of athletes that simply practiced shooting their free throws with those that will only visualize making their free throws. It's fascinating that athletes that only visualize making their free throws are as accurate as those who simply practice making those free throws and in some cases they make more baskets than those who practice only and do not visualize.

You must also know why you are able to achieve your goal. For myself, I had to discover why I was qualified for this position. I looked back at my experience in life and I realized I am an Army veteran with a four year university degree, a leader in my sales career in most positions I have had. I also saw I was in leadership in my local Toastmaster's club. With this experience in mind, I was able to see why I was qualified for this position. I looked at this like David and Goliath in the Bible. When David fought Goliath, he relied on his past experience of killing both a lion and a bear when he was protecting the sheep. This experience gave him the foundation and courage to fight and kill Goliath. I was much like David. My previous experiences in life gave me the foundation I needed so I could run for the United States Senate and see myself winning.

So the question now is, what do you see yourself doing now? I know I am running for office again soon. I can see myself not only running for this office, but I also see myself in office now. What do you see yourself doing?

As you see yourself accomplishing your goal, you must create a plan to achieve your goal as well as a plan of action for accomplishing your goal.

For myself, that meant creating a website where people could learn more about me (www.VoteAndyCraig.com). I also would travel and speak where I could. I would introduce myself and share with them why I was running for the United States Senate and why I would make the best Senator for Oklahoma.

What steps do you need to take to accomplish your goal?

First you need to let people know what your goal is. Making your goal public is key in accountability. I did not let everyone know that I was running for the United States as soon as I made my decision and the news that our senator was retiring early was announced in early January. My wife and I discussed soon after we heard the news, what we were going to do and made our decision that weekend. We knew I was running for the United States Senate, yet it was another 2 to 3 months before we started sharing this goal with everyone. The filing date was April 11, and I started sharing my intention for running about 2 to 4 weeks before this filing deadline. Other candidates made their announcement in January and February. I waited far too long to start letting people know that I was running.

Are you letting people know about your goal? Are you making it public to those who can help you reach your goal? Sharing your dream and your goal with those you are close to increases the likelihood of making your dream or your goal a reality.

One of the challenges you may face as you pursue your goal is explaining to people why your goal is so important.

While I was on the campaign trail, one of my challenges was explaining why I felt the restoration of traditional values was so important to not only Oklahoma, but to the United States.

This wonderful and amazing nation is at a crossroads of returning to the path of our forefathers or a path that a small minority of our population truly desires. This is why I feel we must have restoration of our traditional values.

Our Founding Fathers were very God-fearing men. It is self-evident in their personal writings, as well as in the Declaration of Independence and the United States Constitution.

Two examples of the beliefs of our Founding Fathers:

> *"Our Constitution was made only for a moral and religious people. It is wholly inadequate to the government of any other."* - John Adams

"I have so much faith in the general government of the world by Providence that I can hardly conceive a transaction of such momentous importance [as the framing of the Constitution] ... should be suffered to pass without being in some degree influenced, guided, and governed by that omnipotent, omnipresent, and beneficent Ruler in whom all inferior spirits live and move and have their being." - Benjamin Franklin

Since our nation's founding in 1776, we have come a long way. When we study who our Founding Fathers were, we discover that of the 56 Founders, 29 of them had what would today be considered Seminary Degrees. Not one of them was secular in his orientation (see www.Wallbuilders.com). Based upon this, our Nation was founded upon the precepts found within the Bible. This foundation caused our Nation to flourish and grow, to become the greatest nation in the history of the world. Looking at where we are as a nation today, we have almost divorced ourselves from our founding principles. In 1963, we removed prayer from school, as well as removed Bible reading from school (the irony of this is the first book ever published in this nation was by Congress, and it was the Bible; public schools actually studied the Bible and it was private schools that did not teach from the Bible). What has happened since then is very interesting. The following information comes from the Department of Health and Human Services, Statistical Abstracts from the United States, the Center for Disease Control, and the Department of Commerce, Census Bureau: Since 1963, the number of pregnancies amongst unwed girls ages 15 or younger has risen from 5% in 1963 to 22% as reported in 1991. All data after 1991 reports only for ages 15 to 19. Premarital sex has risen from as low as 5% for age 15 and 22% for age 18, to 27% for age 15 and 70% for age 18. Divorce rates are above 50%. SAT scores (focusing now on education) in 1963 were above 970. SAT scores are now below 900.

These statistics lead me to wonder where we would be if prayer were still allowed in schools?

What are your reasons for achieving your goal? Do you have one or two logical reasons? Maybe you have a list of 10 logical reasons. The real question is whether you have one solid emotional reason for achieving your goal? One emotional heart-felt reason outweighs 10 logical reasons.

I have heard many people talk about wanting to focus on the fiscal issues, only we face as a nation and not deal with the moral issues. However, I do not believe we can do that, I believe our fiscal challenges we face are a direct result of our moral challenges.

Allow me to explain.

> Proverbs 29:2 tell us *"When good people run things, everyone is glad, but when the ruler is bad, everyone groans."*
>
> Hosea 4:6 tells us that, *"People perish for a lack of knowledge."*

We, as a nation, have lost sight of our vision, or should I say, our

The Change 3

true vision. We have vision which is set before us from our leadership. Some good, some need to go back to the drawing board. Our true vision, the reason this nation was founded, has been removed from our sight; the real reason our founding fathers created this nation was for religious liberty.

When we, as a nation, have the correct moral compass, there is nothing that we are not able to do. The Bible tells us in Luke 18:27, "That which is impossible with man, is possible with God."

So, what then, is our vision? Why are traditional biblical values so important? What do traditional biblical values stand for? Traditional biblical values stand for:

- Commitment: Doing what you say you are going to do

- Personal Responsibility: Standing by the choices you make and not blaming someone else for the consequences of that choice

There are many more values I could highlight, but these are two I talked about during my campaign.

Something I believe in is, that life and marriage are the foundation of everything in our nation. Why is life so important for this nation? Life is precious, and it is precious to God. The Bible tells us in Jeremiah 1:5, "Before I shaped you in the womb, I knew all about you. Before you saw the light of day, I had holy plans for you." This is just one verse God tells us how precious life is to Him. He has formed every person ever conceived, and He formed each person with a purpose. When we, as a nation, honor life, we honor God.

With life, there is purpose, and potential. You have a purpose, and potential in your life. This is to help you achieve your potential in your God-given purpose in your life.

This nation was built on purpose and on hope. Life brings hope and purpose and that is why life matters, as well as marriage. Marriage is also the foundation of our nation, because it is the joining of two lives and the creation of a new family and it is the hope of what the future brings. There is much controversy around the definition of marriage and there is much confusion around what marriage really is. Why is marriage so important? And more importantly, why is traditional marriage so important?

Traditional marriage (one man and one woman) has been based upon what is found in the Bible starting with Genesis chapter 1. In these verses, God tells us that He created man in His (God's) image. In Genesis chapter 2, we are told that God created Adam as male. God said it was not good for Adam to be alone, so He created Eve as a female. Eve was created as a companion and helper for Adam. He tells us that man will leave his parents and be joined with his wife and they shall become one flesh.

Why did God tell us that marriage is between one man and one woman? Why is this so vitally important? First and foremost, marriage is about companionship, and two lives coming together and creating a unified life together. The companionship and unity can only be achieved between one man and one woman. Along with companionship and unity, there is procreation, the bringing of new life to this world. These reasons clarify the importance of traditional marriage and why marriage must remain between one man and one woman.

This is how you can achieve your desired dream or goal, which helped me when I ran for the United States Senate.

In summary:

1. Determine your goal or your dream.

2. Know why it is you are achieving your goal or dream.

3. Visualize your end result.

4. Create a plan for achieving your goal.

This is my recent experience in setting my BHAG. Where are you in making your goal and dream a reality?

I trust this information that I have shared with you has been of value to you. If I can be of assistance to you, you can reach me at www.VoteAndyCraig.com

Barbara Swanson

Barbara has been an "eco-preneur" for over 25 years. She has a large networking business and speaks professionally as a business coach and nutritional consultant.

She recently published *Beyond Foods: The Handbook of Functional Nutrition* and is quickly gaining a large audience with this simple, clear communication on a very complex subject.

With a personal network that generates millions in sales yearly, she has worked with literally hundreds of people to help them help themselves through positive life choices - both financially and physically.

The Change Path

By Barbara Swanson

Change is inevitable. From imperceptible daily physical changes to seasonal changes, to the dramatic shifts that are redefining our world climates and economies, change - like death and taxes - is a companion of life.

Yet many - if not most - of us fall into change by default of any planned action, or are thrust into change by outside circumstances.

Some changes cannot be anticipated. A sudden death or an accident can occur to anyone and change life in an instant.

Most of the time, however, change is not sudden. I imagine you - or someone you know - has been or is jobless after being downsized. I am sure you have either experienced or have seen a family deal with a dynamics shift because their children left home for college or a new job.

Sometimes we feel forced into a change by our inability to any longer tolerate current circumstances - a spouse is caught cheating, or drinking yet again, or we are once again passed over for a promotion at our workplace. All of these examples are changes which one could see coming; yet it is the rare person who takes definitive action to control a change before absolutely necessary.

It is really rather astonishing when looked at logically. We are taught how to handle finances and trained for our careers or jobs. We are given a minimum of twelve years education in how to learn and communicate logically and effectively, and at least as many years in "social training" - how to simply get along with others.

Yet while change is a constant of life, most of us have no education on how to recognize the harbingers of change - our personal signals that a change is either needed or coming. These signals are present for everyone, but many are unaware of what they represent. Therefore we never develop a conscious strategy to recognize and take control of change - until it has already arrived.

I certainly have experienced when change controlled me. When unwilling or unable to recognize when a change was necessary or immanent, I had no control over what the change brought to me. I took control over how I chose to react once the change occurred - but many times, I took no actions to control the change itself.

I was clear, from a very young age, that I would not be a victim to circumstances. In order to survive, I learned to make the best of even pretty awful experiences. So it hit me hard when I had a real revelation: I let myself be a victim to the *process* of change. The emotional turmoil and dread that often accompanied major changes in my life were caused in great part by my refusal to be a conscious and active participant until the change was in process and I had no choice left but to get on board. At that point, I would cope and create a life after change - but out of survival mode, not thriver actions.

My "*Aha!*" moment happened about a decade ago, and came about due to my career as a network marketer.

I am fortunate in that I have had great success in this industry (due nearly entirely to the great business people in my large network). I was very comfortable creating service materials (auto-responder letters, conference calls, presentations and even events) - as long as they didn't involve detailed pay plan coaching.

After waiting for nearly twelve months - a year! - for a model of duplication to work with a new pay plan, I was angry, frustrated and tired of watching my network flounder due to a lack of clarity on what to do to achieve duplicable success. It was at that point that I got it: This change needed someone to step up and tackle it head on and I had been waiting for that to be someone else - not me. And I - who prided myself on not being a victim to life - was a victim to this business change.

I decided to learn why I dreaded certain inevitable changes, and how to become proactive with the process of change. As my ability to recognize change signals developed, I realized I could actually drive even unpleasant life changes into the direction I wanted to move.

When I had a surprise and severe health challenge, I discovered that even with unexpected change, the tools I had learned and developed would help me create a life hand-in-hand with change - not just in spite of it.

The Change Sequence diagrams:

- How and why we act or react to change: Our Change Drivers

- The way we notice when a change is needed or coming: Our Change Markers

- How we integrate change into our life: The Change Paths

<u>The Change Drivers</u>

This is the term for what part of your being is driving your *perception* of a change.

Each of us has three different "drivers" that run in the background of life. Each driver has a specific function, and depending on what is going on, will be "in control" over your reactions or actions during this experience. Your ability to access creative energy and choices during times of change are dependent on which driver is "in charge."

The three Change Drivers are:

- The Lower Self
- The Dream Self
- The Higher Self

The Lower Self

The *Lower Self* is aligned with what is also called the ego. While popular belief is that, "ego" describes a person's need to be number one, in actuality, the Ego's job is to keep you safe and sane and to help you establish yourself as an individual. What you define as "you" is most often determined by your Ego.

Your Ego is mainly concerned with keeping your sense of "self" intact. It therefore usually sees any change as a threat to your status quo.

The Dream Self

Your *Dream Self* is the part of you that is connected to your spirit and ego, both. Here will reside your desires, your wishes and dreams. It continually nudges your Ego Self to expand its boundaries of what is safe and wise.

Your Dream Self is urging you to look for something better or more than you currently experience or have. It views change as an opportunity for something more.

The Higher Self

Your *Higher Self* has different names in different religions. It is eternal and able to access higher levels of information and being than does your Ego. Its intelligence nourishes your Dream Self.

Your Higher Self is mainly concerned with helping you evolve a greater understanding of your soul's ultimate goals for this life. It wants to anticipate change so you can direct it in ways that best feed your spiritual growth.

The Change Markers

Change Markers are the signals we receive that change is either needed or immanent. Understanding these signals as they occur is your most important tool in working with change.

The emotional body and unconscious mind of a human are finely tuned to note *everything* going on in our life. In order to stay sane, most of this information remains in our unconscious and we are never even aware it has been recorded.

However, our emotional body is able to sort and connect countless bits of conscious *and* unconscious data and arrange them into patterns. We call this intelligence of our emotional body *intuition*.

When we are open to or in tune with our emotional intelligence, we become aware of these patterns and can choose how to use this information.

Learning to recognize the power of the non-logical, non-intellectual "intelligence" of your emotional body can be life altering. Because our emotional body can connect conscious and unconscious information, it can help us reach conclusions we are not able to construct with our logical intellect. For this reason, it is our emotional body -

our emotions - that first take note of either needed changes, or changes which are coming.

There are three main emotional responses to change. These three responses are your *Change Markers*. Which Change Marker you experience is determined by the Driver that is running your perception of this change.

The Change Paths

There are the three main pathways to dealing with change.

We may use different pathways for differing levels of change. A small change - maybe you need a new computer - is likely to engage a different driver than a major change - for example, if you need to quit your job.

Each Change Path is a reflection of two things:

1. The degree to which you are aware of the needed or coming change. Or in other words, the level at which you are open to and engaged with your intuitive intelligence.

2. The Change Driver in charge of your reaction to the change. The Driver will affect your ability to engage in actions to control the needed or coming change.

CHANGE PATH I: The Change Victim

Change Driver: Ego

Change Markers: Fear/Anger; Avoidance/Anxiety

Change is NEEDED

For many people, this is the default change path. The emotional intelligence change markers by which we are alerted that a change is either acutely needed or is immanent, are present; however, fear is often masked as anger, and avoidance of the issues at hand turns into anxieties.

Because you don't connect to change as the source of the emotional intelligence markers, you are not in control of this change. You are either unconscious of it; or are in denial and refusing to act upon what is coming or already happened - until the change slaps you in the face.

Change Victim Driver: The Ego

The driver of the Change Victim path is the Ego. Because the Ego's job is to keep you safe and intact as an individual, it strongly resists change. This resistance gives rise to fear (what will happen to *me* if this change occurs?) and this fear is often cloaked by anger, then obscured by denial. Because you avoid the source of your feelings, the result is ongoing anger and anxiety. With this dynamic in place, we see a person who gets angry or reactionary to random circumstances: furious because the paperboy missed the porch, or the train was late, or their ride wasn't on time, or the kids are too rowdy. The opposite end is the person who is anxious about everything - when someone is 5 minutes late, if the house isn't neat, if their work isn't in early.

Sadly, rather than protecting the "self" - you - from a potentially devastating change, Ego makes you a Change Victim. If you can't face change, you are left powerless to work with it and minimize any negative results. When we are unable to acknowledge and engage the change, we can only react to how it manifests. The Ego does this because of an insidious pay off - *we are not responsible for what occurs*. Since the Ego's perception of "self" includes self-esteem, avoiding acknowledgement of a change makes sure you are not responsible if anything goes wrong.

A need for emotional safety is nearly an imperative for people with Ego Driver in control. Often, people who walk this change path have strong tapes that run in the back ground convincing them that if they notice change, they will no doubt experience failure at being in control of it. These tapes are unconscious reruns of every experience of failure - even those which are decades old. Being shamed for not getting good grades, being ridiculed for failing at a sport can stay with you for life, leaving you a Change Victim long after the incident is forgotten consciously.

One example of a Change Victim is the person who realizes they are likely to be downsized, but waits until he is unemployed before looking for a new job.

Another example is the person living off of savings who procrastinates on creating a budget or plan of action until there are only months - or weeks - left before she is completely without financial resources.

Bottom line: Avoiding acknowledgement of a pending or needed change never stops it from arriving.

CHANGE PATH II The Change Idealist

Change Driver: The Dream Self

Emotional Change Markers: Aching, Longing, Discontent

Change is DESIRED

The *Change Idealist* is the person who is beginning to wake up to their desire for something "more" in their life. Their emotional intelligence markers signify that change is knocking at their door.

Misunderstood Moods

The Change Path

When you experience an aching for something you cannot put into words... or are discontented in life... it may be your Dream Self informing you of the need and opportunities to welcome and direct a change that will benefit your life. However, quite often these emotional intelligence messages are only tentatively acknowledged, and perceived as just "being ungrateful" for what you currently have. When you don't have the belief to *see* your dreams into reality, your change actions are demoted to daydreams.

If you don't realize that an aching or longing is a signal to look to your dreams, you may dismiss those feelings as just a phase you are going through. If you feel your discontent isn't valid, you may toss away your ideas or desires that don't' fit *what you believe is possible*.

Change Driver: The Dream Self

Most people determine if a dream is appropriate or feasible by their current life circumstances. However, when you free your Dream Self, it will connect to your highest desires - which may not be manifest in your life *at this time*. The secret to working as a Change Idealist is to realize this: *You can never out-perform your own self-image.*

You will never create a life that is out of harmony with what you really believe about yourself. In order to change your life path, you must expand your sense of deserving to the size of your dreams and desires. As you do this, you will experience a yoyo of belief/disbelief in regards to the changes you are dreaming of:

You may feel discontented at work and dream of being your own boss, but fear losing your economic security. You may explore home based businesses, but in your spare time, longing for a change and never committing to one.

Or perhaps you wish for a more fulfilling relationship. You long for more intimacy and consider therapy for your relationship. Then you stay stuck, discontented with your partner, dreaming of more fulfilling intimacy… but refusing to get outside help for fear the relationship may fall apart when examined more closely.

Your Ego Self and Dream Self can seesaw like this and keep you stuck until a change occurs anyway - you are downsized, or your partner leaves. OR - you may take a step towards change and experience the joy of seeing your life move into the direction you want.

In order fully move forward, you have to allow your Dream Self to do something new - trust in change and be a partner with it through deliberate actions based on what you want.

CHANGE PATH III The Change Partner

Change Driver: The Higher Self

Emotional Change Markers: Excitement, Energy, Desire

Change is PLANNED

A *Change Partner* believes that if you can dream it, you can achieve it. They direct life changes according to an ever-expanding understanding of the ideals of their higher self. Change Partners actively seek intuitive messages and use them to help direct their actions.

Change Driver: The Higher Self

A Change Partner is responsible for his choices and knows it. By living according to the intelligence of the Higher Self, she believes she has a message or a purpose, or a wisdom or insight, which is uniquely hers. He knows that when he chooses to face change head-on, the future expands to include change options that further his path towards his highest potential.

Being a Change Partner means you evaluate your life. You are willing to figure out what your soul deeply desires, then set out to make this happen with your life. You don't just ask, "Will this job meet my physical needs?" You ask, "Does this job further my message? Does it give me joy?"

The most important difference between a Change Idealist and a Change Partner is ACTION. When you marry your dreams to belief, then create actions to fulfill those dreams - you are designing your life.

A Change Partner doesn't base his future solely on his current circumstances. As greater understanding and trust in the Higher Self is established, she will learn to see today's circumstances as a bridge to a greater future. If a job doesn't fulfill her deeper mission, she asks, "Does it give me the time to also do what I love? Am I able to use this job to move me towards my ultimate goal?"

SUMMARY

Each year of your life, you are constructing what you become, from change to change. You can design your life… or live it by default.

The Change Victim fears change. He fears that if he tries to work towards a higher calling, he might harm himself at a lower level need (such as income).

The Change Idealist wants more than she currently has. She feels her way into seeing what her life could be… if only she can let go and trust herself and her ability to control the changes necessary to reach the "more" she craves.

The Change Partner has decided to be in control of his life. *He realizes that if you cannot make a living delivering the message you are meant to, it has to be a hobby… and that doesn't have to be his choice.*

How to Move from a Change Victim to a Change Partner

- Practice
    - Always start with what you know you can do (choose a new computer or dishes)
    - Research what you believe you might be able to do (look up jobs online, see what home business are popular)
    - Work your way up to major changes (getting a new apartment, changing your job)
- Be available to ideas
- Take actions that commit to the change you desire
- *Commitment is availability on a daily basis.*
    - Find a network of people that have the same interests and desires and have regular meetings with them
- Remember: If your heart can dream it, your mind can help you create it.

"I have heard several of Barbara's informative and inspirational speeches and am entertained each time. She is a dynamic and charismatic leader with an uncanny ability to relate to everyone regardless of their position or lot in life." - Dr. Rollan Roberts II CEO, Published Author and Professional Business Coach

---

To contact Barbara

541-261-9061

Starhart11@msn.com

For further information and for the Change Path Workbook, visit www.TheChangePath.com

Brian Aubrey Haase

Brian Aubrey Haase is a transgendered master teacher, coach, and speaker, taking his audiences and clients on a journey of self-discovery into their "now." Through powerful workshops, lectures, and coaching programs, Brian helps people overcome their personal obstacles to create the lives they've always dreamed of. He is also getting ready to launch a global organization which stands for human rights in the world.

Brian's quest for answers started over 15 years ago, and has taken him on a journey with many teachers. From studying with Shamans and Gurus, to self-study of religious texts, multiple philosophies, and even consciousness itself, Brian has spent years honing his craft. A gifted healer, Brian is also a Reiki master. He is currently studying with two masters of transformation, learning a new discipline of transformational studies.

Those who he has touched and inspired call him "a true visionary," "authentic," "powerful," "transformational," and "inspirational." His vulnerability and openness create a powerful message about self, and how self also creates the world. Through his unique style of humor, heart, and soulful connection, Brian directs permanent transformation in his clients and audience.

What's Causing "NOW" in Your Life?

By Brian Aubrey Haase

What's happening in your life right now? Before you start reading this chapter, take a moment to check in with yourself. Where are you in your life right now? Is it where you want to be? What do you want in your life that you don't have at this moment? Is it a deep, intimate loving relationship? More money, a better job, or a bigger house? Are you as healthy as you want to be? On a scale of one to ten, with ten being extremely happy, and one being very unhappy, how happy are you in your life right now?

If you said something other than ten, why? Have you ever stopped and wondered what's causing *now* in your life? What's preventing you from having the life of your dreams? And if you're willing to look into it, there is a breakthrough waiting for you. Are you ready to have a breakthrough in your life, and start living in alignment with the life of your dreams? I certainly hope so!

In *The Power of Now,* Eckhart Tolle discusses the importance of living in the now because this is all we have. And while this is true, when we try to practice it, we see the same results we've always seen. We spend days and months trying to "learn" the method that will get us present, and create what we want, and then get frustrated when we don't see results, or even worse, see the same results we've always seen. Why? Because we don't even know that we are not present in our now, even if we are trying to be. And until we discover what's causing *now* in our life, we will not be able to create anything more than what we already have.

In a way, we've already created everything we can create in our lives. That's why our lives are the way they are right now, and not something completely different. That doesn't mean we can't create something else; we can. It does mean, however, that we cannot create something new without being clear on how we created what we already have, and understand that we have to do something, learn something, or try something different to get a different outcome.

What's causing your *now* becomes an important factor in how we respond, and create in the present and in our lives. I've found that people are trying to be present, and live in the present moment, but they are bringing their past with them. They bring in their past experiences as they try to create something new. Then, they're simply operating over old beliefs, and expecting something new. It's like being unhappy, but telling people you are happy. Simply saying things on top of the unhappiness is not the way to be happy. To put it another way, your life is like a house. You've built it to what it is. Your life right now is the house you built. But you want a new house, and you like the lot the house is on, so you want the new house right where the old one is. You don't build another house on top of the one you are living in. In order to build a new house, you have to first deconstruct your old house. Only then can you create the new house you want. Our lives are very similar. We get to deconstruct what we "are," to create what we want to be.

So then, what is our *now* anyway?

Our now is a combination of our experiences, perceptions, thoughts, choices, and the beliefs we have forged from all these things. It is everything we have right now - relationships, jobs, physical health, the way we interact with the world, who we think we are in the world, and the stories we tell ourselves. It's every emotion we have right now, any pain we have in our body, and any thoughts in our head. Your now is just a story of your experiences that you've created as a reality. It's a story you bought into, and in many ways, it appears to be a *fixed* reality. And we make up a lot about it, with some of it working for us, and some against us. *Life is hard, money doesn't grow on trees, no matter how hard I try, it just doesn't work for me, I'm not good enough, not smart enough, not talented enough.* We make up these stories out of our experiences, and we live into them as truth. We create a space in which no other possibility can exist for us, and we become this repeating, perpetual story. Have you ever heard the story of the Titanic? It hits an iceberg and sinks, killing over 1,500 people. Have you ever heard the story of the Titanic where the ship makes it to New York? Of course not! The story ends the same way every time it's told because that's the way it is. If you are living in a story, then it is also being repeated over and over, and we believe it's the way it IS, and most likely we believe it is the way we ARE.

And we will fight with ourselves and others to be right about our story.

Fortunately for us, the remaining chapters of our story haven't been written yet. So imagine if we wrote a story that works for us? What would be possible if there was a twist in plot in our lives? If our story suddenly changed direction? What if we could remove the iceberg from the Titanic story? What if we removed the obstacle that stands between where you are and where you want to be? All the things up until this point still exist, but the way the story is written from here can be anything we want. It can be created for us, by us, no matter what has happened until now.

So what is a belief structure and how do they form?

A belief is simply an idea that we set in stone in our mind. It's what we make up about something, then create it as a truth. Ideas were never meant to be a solid fixture. Ideas are fluid. They are simply what we know as of now. In the book *The Universe in a Single Atom,* The Dalai Lama said, "If scientific analysis were conclusively to demonstrate certain claims in Buddhism to be false, then we must accept the findings of science and abandon those claims." Ideas are not to be set in stone, because at any moment, you may receive new information that could change everything. In the early 1600's, Galileo stated the Earth revolved around the sun, which contradicted the Church who said that the Earth was the center of the Universe. He was tried for heresy, convicted, forced to recant his findings, and lived the rest of his life on house arrest, simply because of a fixed belief structure. And the Church and other astronomers fought to be right about *their* story. Galileo was of course correct, yet so much information was limited due to other's beliefs. Many of the goals we set for our lives are also hindered by our own limiting beliefs.

Beliefs can be formed and taught over generations, or created in a split second. It can be something that someone says to us. Someone saying, "Why do you write those stupid stories" to a little girl who, after breaking through years of doubt about her writing, became a successful and inspirational writer. It can be taught from our parents or caregivers. It can be shown to us from society. It can be an event, or a result of a choice. It can even be thoughts we have about ourselves. And once they become a belief structure, we operate our lives from that.

So how does this prevent us from achieving the life of our dreams?

Well, if I make a choice to start a business, and the business doesn't succeed, I may make up that I'm a failure. If my parents divorce when I'm young, I may make up that I'm not worthy, and I caused the divorce. Or, I may just look in the mirror one day and say that I'm ugly. And if I make up any of these beliefs, then I will always feel like a failure, or that I'm unworthy, or that I'm ugly. And when someone or something tries to show me new information, I will simply live from my beliefs, and push away anything that tries to show me something different. Why? Because I have a belief structure that I have to feed. Anything other than that would be going against my beliefs! And our subconscious will run this program over and over, without us even knowing.

When I was young I didn't know what gender I was, and I made up there was something terribly wrong with me. I made up that no one would love me because of this, so no one could know my terrible secret. Notice I said *I made it up* because this was simply my interpretation. It wasn't told to me, and I had no evidence that no one loved me or that there was anything wrong with me. Consequently, I dealt with a great deal of pain and this entire story became a belief and it became my *now*. I BECAME the painful story when in fact there was nothing wrong with me and plenty people loved me! However, a story is fixed and it lacks possibility and fluidity so there were no other possibilities for me. As a result, when there were opportunities for love, it didn't fit in my belief structure and I turned it away. How could someone love me when there's something wrong with me! So I created failure and loveless relationships because that way it fell right back into my belief structure, which sent away those who loved me, which only reinforced that I wasn't worthy of love. This unconsciously became who I was.

I didn't walk up to people and say "Hi, my name is Brian, there's something wrong with me." But it was my programming.

When you pull up Facebook on your computer, you don't see the thousands of lines of programming that create what you see on the page. You just see Facebook! That's how the stories that operate us work. They're constantly behind the scenes. If these stories were blatantly in front of us, we'd easily shift them! But instead they run us like a computer program. Personally, when I finally realized that the only common denominator in all my failed relationships, in all my pain, in all my circumstances was me, I chose to shift and I became aware that I was the storyteller. There was an awareness of what I was doing to myself, and that the world wasn't actually doing anything *to* me. In that moment, just like you wouldn't build a new house on top of the old one, I didn't create something over what I thought I was. I had to deconstruct what I thought I was, to find out who I am.

I wanted answers. I wanted someone to tell me what to do. And because I had amazing coaches in my life, they never gave me answers. Instead, they created the space for me to find them within myself. Turns out, I was asking the wrong questions. They asked, then gave me the ability to ask myself, the questions that open up self-realization. You have all the answers to what's holding you back in your life, and you can create anything you want. You simply have to start asking the right questions! The questions must look inside of yourself. Nothing outside of you is causing your *now*. It's easy to blame our circumstances, events, and even other people for us not having what we say we want. But when we take control of our own lives, and our own actions, then we free ourselves. Because we will never be able to control what happens outside of us, but we can always control our actions and reactions.

One of the best questions that I coach my clients on is, "What about me?" Not the selfish introverted question, but "what about me" from a responsibility standpoint. It's important to mention that responsibility is not being talked about here as "you did it, blame, shame, right and wrong, or a weight on your shoulders," but as a way of saying, "how am I creating, or how did I create." Because once you see that you are creating something, you can ask yourself, "Is this what I want to create in my life?" And if it isn't, then you can make a choice that is in alignment with what you say you want. How it works is, you ask yourself a question based on what you want answers on. So, as an example, if I wasn't generating the income that I would like to create, I simply ask, "What about me is not creating the income I wish to create?" And then I answer the question. The answer may be "I'm not working as hard as I need to." Notice that it is an inward looking question. It's not about things outside of me. It's not my clients fault, or the economy's fault, or my parent's fault. In fact, it's not fault at all. It's simply a result I have. And you are not your results. You have results, but you are not your results. Being your results, or making the results you have as who you are, will only end up as another belief structure to hold you back.

Now that I have the answer to the first question, I ask it again, only using my last answer as the subject of the next question. "What about me isn't working as hard as I need to?" To which I may answer, "I don't feel confident in what I'm creating right now." Then, ask again using the same formula, "What about me isn't feeling confident?" And I keep doing this over and over, going deeper and deeper into the rabbit hole, until I find the real reason why I'm not creating income. Maybe I end up with the answer that I'm not good enough. Now I have something to work with! Because if I feel that I'm not good enough, then how can anything I do create worth? My results will always fall short of good enough. That's my story! That's my belief structure! And it was all covered up by blaming the economy, or my clients, or who knows what. When we blame others, we say we are helpless in our "now." When we look inward, we are in control of our lives. At this moment I can ask, "Am I willing to be wrong about this story about not being good enough?" And I can look at what I am willing to do. I get to commit to something. Maybe I will write myself an acknowledgement letter of all the things that I have done or accomplished. Maybe I will set some simple, short term goals that I will have success at, to start believing that I am good enough. Whatever it is, the intention is to start to rewrite my story of being unworthy so that I can start achieving what I say I want. But without knowing the underlying story, I will never break free of the results that I have already created in my life, and will continue to create the results I have already, and have always created.

Our conversations with ourselves are powerful. The beliefs we have, that we create, are powerful. If you are in a conversation about lack, then all you will have is lack. If you are in conversation about being unworthy, you will never create worth. Our conversations become our beliefs, and our beliefs become our story, and when we become our story, then the story becomes our results. And while we will have varying levels of success in our lives, it will always be connected to the story we tell. When you are sick of the story, and when you are willing to give the story up, to be wrong about the story, you will be able to create something new. In that space, you can create your vision. Then, you start making commitments based on your vision. Because you will either be committed to your vision, or your story. If you choose to look deep inside of yourself, if you choose to be wrong about your story, and if you are willing to commit to a different outcome, then you will start seeing something new. When you commit to your vision, you take committed action in alignment with your vision. With committed action, you will begin to see results that you never have before. And when your story comes up, use the tools in this chapter and find a coach to support you. A simple plan for success is to have a vision of what you want, take committed action that is in alignment with that vision, add accountability to stay on track, and you will start seeing incredible results in your life. Accountability is key. It's why people get trainers when they go to the gym. Because a coach or trainer will take you past the places where you normally stop. They also give you the tools to get the results you want to have. Because if you had the tools already, you would have created what you want by now. And they have that new information that may just change your belief structure. The only question left is, are you ready to have extraordinary results in your life? Because the life you want is possible. And it's possible right now.

What's Causing "NOW" in Your Life?

To contact Brian:

888-406-1701 Ext 1

brian@brianhaase.com

www.brianhaase.com

www.facebook.com/thebrianhaase

twitter: @thebrianhaase

www.youtube.com/thebrianhaase

www.linkedin.com/in/thebrianhaase

Carol Look, LCSW, EFT Master

Carol Look is an author, speaker, coach, and creator of her signature coaching method, *The Yes Code.* She is a founding **EFT Master** and has been a pioneer and leading voice in the **EFT (Tapping)** community for 18 years. She is known for combining her distinguished background in traditional psychotherapy with energy medicine for unprecedented innovations in the application of **EFT**.

Carol is a highly sought after international speaker and workshop leader. She has taught workshops in Australia, France, England, Brussels, Canada, and all over the United States. She is also a frequent guest on the leading Global Telesummits, reaching thousands of people with her work. She authored the popular books: ***Attracting Abundance with EFT***, ***The Tapping Diet*** and ***Stop Feeling Lazy: How to Eliminate Procrastination Once and For All***. She is featured in the leading **EFT** documentaries as an Energy Therapist Expert.

Find Your Next Yes

By Carol Look, LCSW, EFT Master

Have you ever made decisions in your life based on someone else's feelings?

Do you sometimes feel confused about whether to say "yes" or "no" to opportunities that are presented to you?

Have you ever felt as if you were living someone else's dream?

Happiness will be elusive as long as you are unable to find your own "yes" to questions, decisions, or options you are presented with throughout your daily life. Every decision is important, even the ones that seem small or inconsequential. And if you don't know how to plug into your own "yes" or "no" answers, then you won't be able to live the life of *your* dreams.

My job is to help people like you *create a life you love, one yes at a time.* Luckily, this is my passion as well.

Identify Your Blocks

The first step to creating a life you love is to identify your emotional blocks. What gets in the way of making the best decisions for yourself in order to live the life of your dreams? You need to be clear, congruent and aligned in order to make the right decisions. In other words, your head, heart and gut need to be in agreement so that you know when you say "yes" you are truly meaning "yes." There is no maybe about it. And the only decision that is "right" is the one you feel completely congruent about.

As a success coach, I routinely invite my clients to go deeper into their truth, find authenticity and live a congruent life – a life where your head, heart and gut are all aligned. But you can't live an authentic life when you can't *Find Your Next Yes*... You'll be living someone else's life and the result is sad, draining and exhausting. From my personal experience, I know how painful this can be.

Learning how to *Find Your Next Yes* is challenging and takes practice. The good news is that it is totally within reach of anyone who is willing to take the time to develop these skills. Are you ready?

So in order to be able to *create a life you love, one yes at a time*, you need to eliminate any emotional blocks you might have to being clear in your heart and mind so you can answer "yes" or "no" whenever you are presented with challenges, questions or decisions.

Most people have numerous emotional or energetic blocks to getting clear answers to small conflicts or daily decisions. And being at any significant crossroad is even more challenging if being clear is difficult or foreign. Why? Some of us were taught to deny or ignore our deepest feelings. Others were taught that it is unsafe to have a different viewpoint. And still others never learned how to find their own center, so when faced with choices, they are driven by their fears and impulses.

Understanding Sabotage

Clients often engage in coaching packages with me because they are tired of sabotaging themselves – they procrastinate constantly at work or they're late for important meetings. They pick fights with loved ones, they engage in avoidance behavior, their perfectionism makes them emotionally paralyzed, or they find themselves rebelling against their boss. When you're sabotaging yourself, being able to *Find Your Next Yes* feels hopeless.

While I have no doubt that you want to stop the sabotage behavior, did you know that you need to heal your *fear of being clear* about making important decisions? Most clients expect me to coach them on being more organized, having priorities and making the right "to do" lists. They aren't prepared to consider that their fear of being clear is the culprit, or that there might be positive consequences to their sabotage behavior.

Think about it: if you aren't clear – when there's static in your vibration or thought process because of fear – you will not get where you want to go, no matter what action steps a coach suggests to you. There are simply too many invisible blocks.

You might be asking: *why would I keep sabotaging myself?* Good question! Let's explore that. Sabotage is only a symptom of an emotion or belief that is blocking you. Sabotage is a definable and frustrating behavior by itself, but it is *fueled by specific fears*. My personal and professional experience has taught me that *Finding Your Next Yes* is nearly impossible when deep fears are present.

When you notice that you are sabotaging yourself, I recommend looking at your behavior in a new way. Instead of criticizing yourself saying, *"there I go again..."* try looking at your procrastination or perfectionism as a *solution to a problem*, rather than the problem itself. A sabotage behavior such as procrastination is actually solving a problem for you by protecting you from an outcome you fear or want to avoid. When you uncover what you're afraid to face, you can clear the emotional conflict and start to behave in accordance with your values and desires. Your "yes" will then be crystal clear to you.

There are two primary topics that surface when sabotage blocks my clients from being able to *Find Their Next Yes*: they are either suffering from a *fear of failure* or a *fear of success*. Most of their self-sabotage behavior has been created to protect them from failing or succeeding.

Do you know which fear fuels your own sabotage and blocks you from being able to *Find Your Next Yes*? If you have a *fear of failure*, you won't want to write your book, finish your website, lose the weight or enter a relationship because you are convinced you'll be criticized and fail… again. If you have a *fear of success*, you will be focused on how other people will react to your success, how unsafe it is to be visible, and you will work very hard to sabotage yourself so you don't have to shine and be a target of envy.

Ask the Right Questions

It's essential to ask the right questions when you are out of alignment with how you want to live your life. To get to the bottom of why you are blocking yourself from creating a life you love, you need to understand *why* you would choose self-sabotage... My two favorite questions about any block or sabotage behavior are:

(1) What is the "upside" of sabotaging yourself?

(2) What is the "downside" of being successful?

For example, if you're procrastinating on big decisions at work or at home, ask yourself this question:

- **What's the "upside" of sabotaging yourself?** (How does it help you to play small?)

Think of this in terms of a *fear of failure*. While I've had clients respond with a wide variety of answers, they all had to agree that there was an "upside" to sabotage and a "downside" to being clear in their lives. They readily admitted that blocking themselves from making a decision actually protected them from an outcome they didn't want to face or a fear they anticipated. Self-sabotage was just the behavior; the underlying feeling was a *fear of failure*. So the sabotage had an "upside" – it actually protected them from the risk of failing.

See if you can relate to the reasons some of my clients have sabotaged themselves in their relationships, at work, and with their health. (These responses are to the question: **"What is the upside of sabotaging yourself?"**)

- Relationships:
    - Clients often report that if they are very successful, it would upset the balance in one of their primary relationships (partner, parent, or close friend.) So they feel compelled to sabotage themselves by being unclear.
    - *Are you afraid that being clear will "rock the boat" in one of your relationships?*
- Professional Success:
    - Clients often reveal that they fear other people's reactions to their success, so they sabotage themselves at work. (Consider how your colleagues might treat you if you get promoted or double your annual income…)
    - *Are you afraid to "rock the boat" at work?* That may be why you hold back, play small, or sabotage your own success.

- If you keep the peace by not changing any dynamics in your professional relationships, no one will be upset.

- Sabotage behavior such as procrastination keeps you from being professionally successful. *(Is an "upside" to sabotaging yourself feeling more emotionally safe?)*

- Health:
  - Clients often reveal that they are afraid to make a commitment to physical health (losing weight, starting an exercise program, following a self-care plan) because their improvement might make other people jealous or envious. So they sabotage their bodies.
  - *Does your fear of success get in the way of physical health?*

Now get to the bottom of your sabotage from another angle. If you are frustrated because you can't be clear and feel stuck in some aspect of your life, ask yourself my other favorite question:

- **What is the "downside" of being more successful?** (What consequences might you fear if you are really successful?)

Again, over more than two decades of working as a traditionally trained psychotherapist, EFT Master and life coach, clients have revealed fascinating responses to this question in the following areas:

  - Relationships:
  - The "downside" of being more successful helps clients "keep the peace" in their primary relationship. If

they let the other person be in charge of making all the decisions, nothing has to change.

- Being unfocused allows them to avoid confrontation on "hot topics" at home. *(Do you avoid discussing heavy topics with your partner for fear it may cause too much friction?)*

- Not being decisive or successful protects them from criticism. *(As long as you don't take a stand, you can't be criticized for it.)*

- Professional Success:

  - Being more successful feels unsafe and too visible. Being too successful means they can't be invisible or protected from other people's reactions.

  - Being too successful would mean they had to come out from under the radar. *(You can't play small when you're successful.)*

    - Staying "under the radar" means no one will notice or ask too much of them.

    - Playing small helps them hide emotionally, so they feel safe from judgment. *(The downside of being more successful is emotional danger.)*

- Health:

  - Sabotaging their health keeps them stuck.

- If they were clear, committed and congruent, they would move forward… and there are always consequences of moving forward!

- *Does being stuck allow you to "relate" to your friends with similar issues? While being successful would feel lonely?*

    o Being too successful means they won't might have to "live up to" other peoples' expectations.

    o Being unsuccessful means they don't have to take responsibility for their lives through good health and vitality. *(Does taking responsibility for your health feel overwhelming, difficult, or challenging?)*

Do you recognize yourself in any of these examples?

Remember, the behavior you are doing – procrastination, being late, making mistakes – is actually *solving a problem for you*. And if you want to find out the real reason you are sabotaging your success, keep asking yourself my favorite questions regarding your work, your relationships and your health:

- ***What's the "upside" of sabotaging my success?***

- ***What's the "downside" of being more successful?***

When you find the answers to these questions, you are a long way towards your goals of personal and professional success. You can use a variety of energy techniques (EFT / Tapping is my favorite) to clear your fears once you've identified what they are. For example, if you're afraid of completing your project because you might be criticized, now you know *why* you've been procrastinating and can clear this emotional conflict. You're not a bad person, you're not lazy, you're just afraid of someone else's reaction.

If asking yourself these questions revealed that you're afraid to finish writing your book because you suspect your success will "rock the boat" in one of your professional relationships, then you know the reason behind your behavior. When you know the reasons you sabotage yourself, you can eliminate the emotional conflicts and move forward with ease and grace.

Once you have cleared your *fear of failure* or your *fear of success*, you will have the emotional room to hear and feel your "yes" and "no" signals from your deepest internal guidance – your heart.

Practice Receiving Your "Yes" and "No"

Do you know what a "yes" or "no" answer feels like from inside of you? We have so often been told what we should think, what we should feel, and how we should behave, that the simple art of knowing what a "yes" or "no" feels like has been lost!

First, your mind and body need to be still and quiet enough to retrieve the answers you are generating. Once the static has died down and you can actually hear or feel your answers from inside, then you need to recognize the difference between a "yes" or "no."

When I was first developing my own methods to living with deep congruence, I was surprised to learn that my "no" answer was really a confused internal reaction full of static. I had expected my "no" answer to be particularly loud and definite, but it wasn't. And my "yes" answer was incredibly peaceful, calm and quiet. Undeniable, but quiet. And I hadn't expected that either. So keep an open mind when you're searching for your own "yes" or "no" – your energy system might surprise you!

I invite my clients and workshop participants to practice discerning their "yes" or "no" on a regular basis on small and seemingly inconsequential issues. In my professional and personal experience, if you are unable to make a clear decision about what to wear to the meeting or eat for lunch, you won't be able to distinguish between a "yes" or "no" on the bigger decisions in life!

Here's a simple exercise to practice getting your personal "yes" or "no" answers: Think about your favorite color – feel that feeling inside, the stillness, the joy – that's a simple "yes." Now think about something you find very unappealing - a color or pattern - and feel how different that feels inside of you. That reaction represents a simple "no."

Now repeat this exercise while thinking of your favorite person (or pet) in the world. Remember interacting with them, having fun, enjoying yourself – and notice the feelings inside of you and the pleasure and joy in your mind – that's a simple "yes." Now, think of someone who really bothers you, someone you don't trust or like. That feeling you are getting inside of you when you think of someone you mistrust is a simple "no" answer. (You can also try the exercises while placing your right hand over your heart center to see if you get any additional guidance.)

After quieting down all your fears by asking the right questions and uncovering whether you have a *fear of failure* or a *fear of success*, you were able to practice hearing and knowing what a "yes" or "no" feels like to you. Now, you will be able to listen in to your heart and locate the "yes" or "no" answer to all the important, critical conflicts or decisions in your life.

Think of a request someone has made of you, an opportunity you're not sure about, or some options about a new direction in your life. Be as still and quiet as you can be. Now "go inside" and see if you can recognize a "yes" or a "no" about this decision. If you hear and feel more fear, you can go back and ask yourself the two questions I listed earlier:

(1) What is the "upside" of staying stuck or sabotaging yourself?

(2) What is the "downside" of becoming more successful?

Clear the fears that are fueling your sabotage behavior with an energy method (EFT/ Tapping, for example), journaling, coaching or whatever method you prefer. Now you will be able to go inside again and "retrieve" your "yes or "no."

Make a Habit of Expressing Gratitude

Once you have your "yes" answer about the project, the direction you want to go, or your relationship, then sit with it - does it feel right? Do you feel totally congruent? Did you get a true "yes" as your answer?

Before you take any action, I recommend you infuse your decision with the energy of gratitude and appreciation. If you don't feel gratitude for the answer you received and the action you need to take, I consider this worthy feedback from your heart that you're not quite ready to move forward. There may be another fear to eliminate.

Write a gratitude list about a specific situation, relationship or project you've been struggling with in your life. Feel appreciation and gratitude about the decision you've made until you're truly ready to take the necessary action. When you tune into the action you are about to take and feel 100% grateful about this opportunity or situation, you are ready to move ahead.

Too often people are impulsive – they feel a fleeting emotion and act on it right away. They haven't cleared their fears around a true yes, and don't feel genuinely grateful for the situation, so they aren't emotionally aligned. When you are ready to take the right action, you will feel full of gratitude, love and appreciation, and it will feel easy and joyful to make the right decisions.

Once you know how to *Find Your Next Yes* in any situation, you can start to *create a life you love, one yes at a time.*

Enjoy the journey!

In addition to training and mentoring energy practitioners worldwide, Carol runs a **Certified Abundance Coaching Program** for practitioners who are passionate about coaching others to lead lives of exceptional success. For more about Carol, please visit http://www.carollook.com.

Eden Adele

Eden Adele – Evolutionary relationship specialist, best-selling author, highly sought-after speaker, and affectionately known as the *Premiere Passionator*. Through the *SatisFillment* intimacy evolution system she created, she instills practical guidelines and direction into the active living routines of those who are severely deprived of intimacy and suffering emotional disconnect. After more than 30 years engaged in personal research of varying industry experts, interviews, and objective findings, Eden has distilled valuable, solution-based guidelines and instruction specifically indicated for her constituent audience. Fearlessly bold in her potpourri of offerings, Eden provides an arsenal of intimacy-expanding exercises for singles and couples. Through her *Get Back to Passion Institute*, Eden provides a generous range of service products for marriages, couples, and individuals for the express purpose of intimacy rejuvenation. Whether in self-paced online action plans or live retreat intensives and everything in between – she has techniques sure to guide your lost desire back to lasting intimacy. If you're willing, then don't miss Eden's vehicle of success for passionate, loving relationships and marital unions. It will be the ride of your life both figuratively and literally!

Are You Doing What You Know Or Do You Know What You're Doing?

Eden Adele

Did you realize that the greatest blessings in the areas of intimacy and passion you're going to experience in your entire life are ahead of you and require *your* participation in their sacred co-creation? You can create deeper levels of connection with your mate by first doing the work to reconnect to your own satisfaction and fulfillment. I call it s*atisfillment*. Satisfillment is the new sexy!

Achieving satisfaction (outward) and fulfillment (inward) is often thought to be an 'either/or' proposition. However, satisfillment is also an actual process that will guide you into having both simultaneously. As a result, your mindset will produce a lifestyle of power, passion, and peace of mind. You will magnetize intimacy, passion, and love – even if you're currently single. If you're in a relationship, your expressions of intimacy can have the intensity, adventure, and the heat of your dreams. In this chapter, you will learn the single thing that must be right in your mind before you can be satisfilled. It's the one thing that if you get it wrong, there's no getting anything else right enough to compensate. Get it right and you can love passionately, instead of just reading about it.

How do I know? Like a lump of coal that becomes a precious diamond, I've known intense pressure and considerable refinement. I share the most critical lessons of those experiences so you don't have to go that route to get to effortless satisfillment. There was nothing sexy about my long road back to passion. However, I emerged on the other side with pearls and direction that enable me to guide you, as I've done with so many others, to get there for yourself. And, trust me - you want to get there. More on that later.

Chances are, you're skeptical.

After all, actually living that level of intimacy and passion goes against practically everything you've been programmed to believe. And even though that programming led you right to the heart of the pain, dysfunction, and toxicity that made you pick up this book – you're just doing what you know. Now, it's time to know what you're doing. Only then can you create the transformation that will take your intimacy to new levels.

As dismal as your outwardly good, inwardly empty life may feel to you, know that the intimacy waiting for you can be an absolute erotic amusement park compared to the purely sexual playground you've been dutifully enduring (instead of wildly enjoying) until now. I know this from personal and professional experience and years of active learning that I now use to teach others to achieve satisfillment.

It's so much easier to do what you know, than it is to know what you do.

Digest that simple, profound truth for a moment. Your life is exactly as it is primarily because you're doing what you know – not necessarily because you know what you're doing. *Awake* and *aware* are different by more than just one letter.

The soundtrack of your heartache has been blaring in your life too long. Calling the shots and taking control. Time for satisfillment. Even if as a young child your parents didn't demonstrate a loving relationship, you can still experience a passionate, trusting and intimate relationship with your mate - now or in the future. Satisfillment. Even if your young (or not so young) self was sexually violated - molestation, date rape - name the assault - you can have the most satisfilling intimacy of your life, **even** if you're over 40.

Weighed down by the sometimes overwhelming responsibility of being the custodial parent? Or being the primary caretaker for critically ill parents? You, too, can reinvent yourself into the absolute best you've ever been.

Are you *awake* or *aware*? Have you been *aging* or *saging*? Awake is aging. It's inevitable. Whatever way you were taught to walk through the world as a youth has since been the bedrock of your every life choice. Aging only increases access to more ways to repeat the pathologies of your early programming. Since you lacked the capacity for awareness of the Divine truth of you, you thought you were growing up when you were simply growing older. You were aging, not saging. Saging is aware. It's proactive. It's consistently challenging faulty paradigms and replacing them with new perspectives on love, life, and the world around you. Saging is the spice that may be truly missing from your life.

Fast forward a few decades, through several years of education, career, marriage, children - the most consuming responsibilities and accountabilities of your life. You followed the common program that valued emotional suppression over expression. You played by the rules. You did what was expected. Yet you woke up one day with a profound awareness of an endless emptiness. It's a hole in your soul reminding you that this life you've built, these choices you've made, have landed you smack in the middle of 'how-in-the-wide-world-did-I-end-up-here-ville!'

So very far from that one thing. You're not satisfied or fulfilled, especially in your intimate life. Despite being a *good* person, you still try to control or manipulate your way into love or through the love you already have. That emptiness mentioned before makes it nearly impossible for you to fully engage your sensuality or even embrace the imperfect perfection of your own body. The persistent, crippling messages of being fundamentally unlovable only make it worse. It's likely that you often put others before yourself, value their feelings above yours, and sacrifice to meet their needs at the expense of your own - especially at the expense of intimacy and passion. You crave both, but like me so many years ago, you haven't yet identified that path to satisfillment. Worse, we take paths falsely marked as instruction in intimate, passionate behavior.

For too many, porn has directly or indirectly been the primary sex instructor. Television, movies and videos are also culprits. Such that, now you're only comfortable with putting Tab A into Slot B because there are no sex scenes for transcendence, for Divine sacred 'soulgasm' - for connecting hearts, not merely parts. And so you lie inches away from your mate dreading the next failed attempt at multi-orgasmic pleasures or new position fantasies. While still oblivious to the truth that the best path to those delicacies is directly through the heart of what porn, and the other visuals, never taught you; of what your violation never left behind.

Violation takes many forms. For instance, growing up, I quickly learned that the people I most depended on would often let me down. Take my parents. I had a front row seat to their disillusionment - overwhelmed by the stress of their unfulfilled dreams and the pressures of life in general. When they fought, my five-year-old self took it personally. Consequently, I felt off balance and out of place, tolerated and not celebrated in my own home; despite being well-dressed, well-fed, presented with celebratory gifts and going on vacations. It's difficult to recall a time as a child that either of their eyes lit up when I entered the room.

Are You Doing What You Know Or Do You Know What You're Doing?

I believed I was the real reason my father left. My mother was emotionally unavailable much of the time. Still, I became a people-pleasing machine for fear that she, too, would leave. I could not take another physical abandonment. Given all of the above, how could I then have a comfortable place in the world? How could I avoid internalizing the blame, even into adulthood?

Many of you can likely relate to the toll that physical and emotional abandonment took. Losing my first love devastated me, caused me to drop out of college where I had been on the Dean's list. Another man who 'loved' me, left me. Sound familiar? My now superior people-pleasing skills helped me do whatever it took to 'save' a series of doomed relationships. As you can imagine, every one of them ended. Finally, I became proactive and began to seriously study human behavior. I believed that if I could at least understand the why's of what people did in the name of love and relationships, I would learn what to avoid, and 'make' men want to stay with me.

My research found that it basically boiled down to this: men ultimately married women they found physically attractive and that they connected to emotionally. Not exactly brain surgery. The attractive part is self-explanatory, but how do you engineer that emotional connection? One way is by taking the risk of sharing my vulnerability with them. Then they knew they would be safe doing the same with me. I was on a mission to be what they wanted and who they needed. I was already genuinely interested, caring and concerned, so it was easy for me to do.

These connections were no accident. I had no magic. Everything was purely intentional. I absolutely, unequivocally and consciously lived as the best version of myself. This meant several great relationships. Unfortunately, most people are accustomed to drama and chaos. Consequently, being in a truly serene and caring relationship is foreign to them. While they enjoy it initially, they typically become quite uncomfortable because they don't know what to do.

Drama they know. Serenity, not so much. I didn't raise my voice when they expected screaming. I expressed my anger without name calling or belittling. I sought information when they expected interrogation. My approach to problem solving was to fix the problem, not to fix him. Ultimately, however, their desire to be comfortable would often override the desire to be in a relationship – at least with me. So when they returned to the familiar, I wasn't surprised. Hurt, but not surprised.

The lesson I still needed to learn was how to create effective emotional boundaries. My early abandonment left a 'brain stain' that governed my world for many years. That stain was the reason I stayed far too long in relationships where I was giving my *everything* when they were just giving me their *something*. Lesson learned.

I rose above any negative perceptions and kept a positive attitude. I refused to make my traumas the benchmark by which I measured all men.

How did satisfillment release me? Satisfillment is the process that brought the rain to my brain stain. It was time for a new ruler on my heart's throne. That long ago heart pain cannot remain where true love reigns. Step-by-step, my Divine strategy unfolded. I kept progress journals that became the blueprint that allows me to share my lessons with others. It's amazing how God can redeem your pain and turn it into power, passion, and peace of mind – when you allow it.

As you learn to get clear and strong in your intention, keep in mind that it's a process. And like all things of substance, it takes effort. Like everyone else, I'm a work in continuous progress. *Progress, not perfection* is my mantra for life.

I experienced the best and worst of times in my 40's. I got married at 40 (only marriage to date) to a man nearly 12 years my junior who wasn't the genetic father of my then nine-year-old daughter. He is the only father she's ever known. As often happens in relationships, financial issues dealt our relationship a serious blow. I was the only financial contributor for years. Adding to the financial issue, my mother was diagnosed with Alzheimer's and about a year later, came to live with us. The bank foreclosed on the house I paid for, the home business failed and, at the advice of my attorney, I filed Chapter 13 bankruptcy – twice – to stall the sale of the house.

My mother declined to the point of needing round-the-clock care, at least during the day. I found a day care program. Several months in, I discovered my husband was having an affair with one of the program's administrators. She wasn't his only one, but she was the pregnant one. At least that what she told me.

I asked my husband to leave. I needed time and space to process this feeling of being blindsided by an 18-wheeler. My daughter was nearly inconsolable in his absence. She adored him and threatened to run away to find him. My unwise choice had already denied her one father. I didn't have the heart to deny her two. All of this took a toll on my health.

Can you imagine having to manage a thyroid condition, high blood pressure, anxiety and mood swings? Or, being in the ER twice a month over a three-month period with panic attacks? Of course, my doctors had a pill for all my ailments - SEVEN medications in total.

In the midst of it all, I was determined to save my marriage. My background made divorce an absolute last resort. Maybe it wasn't the best decision, but it was the best I could make at the time. We only lasted another three years.

I also lost my job during this time and lived on unemployment for two years. When that ran out, I was on public assistance for several months before I found another full-time job. My car was impounded for unpaid parking and expired tags tickets mostly courtesy of my husband. Impound fees or my daughter's college tuition? The car was repossessed.

So due to all of the above, I determined there was a critical question that needed an honest answer. The question that gets you to the one thing that you must get right in order to live the love - and the life - of your dreams. The one thing that if you get it wrong, there's no getting anything else right enough to compensate.

Simply put, that question is: how will you define yourself from now on?

I felt as if that question had been Divinely burned into the fibers of my soul. No matter how horrible the drama and the trauma you've been through, it's time to redefine yourself. In doing the work, I dedicated an entire year to uncovering the specific answer to that question for myself. I journaled. I took classes. I cried. I prayed. I researched. I saw doctors. Rinse and repeat. Most importantly, I was gut-wrenchingly honest with myself about myself. I consciously identified my weaknesses, embraced my flaws and celebrated my strengths. In the process, I was liberated from the pressure of meeting unreasonable expectations of myself – even when those expectations were mine.

A pivotal realization concerning my marriage is actually a truth many others are still living. I realized I'd become the consummate liar. I lied with my life. I lied to my husband about what I honestly expected from him. I pretended things didn't bother me that cut me to my core. I shut down sexually; turned off and disconnected from most feminine things about me. I made promises about being more intimately engaged in my marriage that I knew I didn't have the heart to keep. I rationalized that I would just 'woman up' and do it because it was the promise I made at the altar. I didn't. There were periods when we went months without physical intimacy because I was in an emotional abyss. There is truly no deception as thorough or blinding as self-deception.

I was doing what I know, but I didn't know what I was doing. I was awake, not aware. I was aging, not saging.

Doing the work to finally define myself for myself by myself – irrespective of all other relationships, attachments, and expectations (including my own) – was the single sexiest thing I've ever done. How did I do the work?

- By admitting and accepting that only I was responsible for how I showed up in my relationships

- By accepting that my past did not dictate my future – positive or negative

- By committing to stay in the process to reprogram my thinking in order to finally own my power, my passion and my peace of mind

- By creating a specific action plan that allowed me to do this process in bite-sized chunks; a simple, effective, repeatable pathway to my essence

- By expanding my concept of sexual expression to include all areas of my life, irrespective of my relationship status

NOW I know what I'm doing. NOW I decide who and how I am. NOW I choose how I share the Divine radiant brilliance that is uniquely me. I've stopped adjusting my shine to accommodate others. I'm comfortable in my imperfectly perfect skin, embracing of every joy and sorrow of my past, and determined to live the rest of my life as the best of my life. I experience the beauty of authentic intimacy and passion, whether or not I'm in a relationship.

And all is well – because I'm aware, not just awake. Saging, not just aging. I know what I'm doing instead of just doing what I know.

I am satisfilled. And the BEST news is – you can be, too. For the sake of your own satisfillment, I pray that you do.

To contact Eden:

Be sure to visit her website to become a part of the global SatisFillment evolution. http://www.edenadele.com

Nina Boski

Nina Boski is an entertainment and media executive and host, lifestyle expert and coach, author, facilitator and entrepreneur.

Getting her start in radio, Nina expanded into many areas of media. As an entertainment and lifestyle expert, Nina was a TV correspondent for the Hallmark Channel's "New Morning" show, as well as LIME's Healthy Living Channel (now GAIAM TV). She has also been on air on Lifetime TV as well as the WE network interviewing celebrities for entertainment features. Nina currently hosts her own radio show and has aired LifeBites radio on Sirius Satellite Radio and AOL Radio, and is a main contributor for *Positively Positive*, the inspirational social media smash with over two million followers, and Australia's *Make the World Move*. More recently she hosted and produced a weekly TV show on emPOWERme TV "LifeBites LIVE!"

Nina's passion for life is evident the moment she walks into a room. With a unique combination of self-help and entertainment, she combines her media world with helping people as a lifestyle expert. She is also the co-author of a book for women, called the *Spirit of Women Entrepreneurs and her new upcoming book, Rock On With Your Wonderful Bad-Ass Self (Dec 2015)*. Her media savvy and experience has earned her a loyal following and national & international recognition as a lifestyle and entertainment host and coach. Nina is also producing her first feature film, *Goodnight Marily*

Rock On With Your Wonderful Bad-Ass Self

By Nina Boski

"If you want to be successful in life, stop asking for permission." - Anonymous

Definition of bad·ass,
>   noun
>   - ❖ "A dynamic, confident, take charge, ready for a challenge person."
>   - ❖ "Belief in one self. Fearless; will not cower under adversity."
>   - ❖ "Comfortable in one's skin. Connected to oneself."
>   - ❖ "Ready to take on the world and enjoying the ride."

If you are reading this book, and specifically this chapter, you are ready for a change and wanting to become a wonderful bad-ass yourself. Now, you may be very clear about what kind of wonderful bad-ass you would like to become, or you may just have a fuzzy inclination that something profound is stirring deep within you. Wherever you are, it is time to ask yourself two important questions to get you started on your adventure:

1. Are you ready for the change?

2. Are you going to be successful in your change?

The Change 3

For me, I have always been a risk taker. I love change and opportunity to create new things. Innately, I am a positive person and people see the positive in me. However, like many of us, my filter from an early age was programmed not to succeed. Although my mom and family loved me, they did not always fill my mind and heart with thoughts of, "You can do it." They didn't have big expectations for my future, but I always had big dreams. It's through the twists and turns of falling down and getting up, through failing and succeeding, that I learned I could be successful in life. I learned it's not just having the will to change, but the will to evoke, create, ignite, excite and be passionate about really becoming a wonderful, bad-ass self!

> *"We cannot solve our problems with the same thinking we used when we created them."* – Albert Einstein

I see many people in my coaching practice, and out in the world, who think that they are going to make a change with the same old energy and don't take new action. They are waiting for some Divine inspiration. If you want to create a change, you need to start embodying that change now. No more waiting! People say, "I want to start working out," but they haven't even put on their tennis shoes. They are only in thinking mode. Or, you hear some say, "I want to make more money," but they have not implemented one new strategy in order to shift the energy. Thinking about putting something into action and actually putting something into action are two different things. In order to rock on with your wonderful bad-ass self, you need to get crystal clear and not just talk change. Be the change – NOW!

> *"It is in your moments of decision that your destiny is shaped."* -— Tony Robbins

Once you know you are ready, willing, and able, you'll start to shift, as long as you put it into motion. But, just like with anything in life, before you get moving, it is important that you have a vision. A vision gives your life direction and a concrete place to grow into. In my life, vision was never the issue, but creating a grounded structure and support system was always my stumbling block. After leaping without a proper support system in place, and suffering the bumps and bruises from it, I got a clue – maybe I need to do it differently. If you do not couple your vision with focus and structure, it is like jumping off a diving board with no water in the pool. You'll crash and, believe me, it will hurt. Vision is key in becoming a wonderful bad-ass, but building a structure will allow the freedom and the support to manifest that delightful dream!

> *"In order to carry a positive action, we must develop a positive vision."* – Dalai Lama

One of the first things you want to do before embarking on your bad-ass adventure is to get clear about what it is you want to create. I meet with so many people who have not developed a meaningful vision for themselves. They'll say, "I want to make a career change." I'll ask, "Do you know what kind of change you want to make?" or "What are you passionate about?" Their response, "I don't know." If you are going to rock on with your wonderful bad-ass self, you will need to go deeper in order to expand who you are, what you want, and what you need to get there. Vision needs focus, clarity, and structure in order to fully come to life! Part of being a wonderful bad-ass is not being afraid to set the stage for yourself to fully bloom. In fact, you should be excited about creating a plan for blooming and taking calculated risks. The key is to create a solid foundation that allows you to fully manifest that change. The bottom line, "KNOW THY SELF."

> *When opportunity knocks, are you prepared enough to go for it?* - Anonymous

Don't get me wrong. Sometimes great things can happen unexpectedly. I love to follow my impulses and act on my ideas, and sometimes creating as you go can help to overcome inhibitions and can be the best way to manifest an opportunity. If you find yourself in this place, then jump in and fill in as you go – dream, structure, get it clear and focused, all while you are in the process of creating, but don't skip calculating the risks and creating that foundation. The key to getting this energy to really work for you is to pull in the right people and support to help you make the change or build your dream. So many times we have big dreams, but we don't have the right resources, time or systems to make it happen. Don't let this be you or you will be that person who dives in without any water in the pool. Don't take on risky opportunities if you know you can't pay the rent at the end of the month. Part of being a wonderful bad-ass is being smart enough to know what choices to make.

> *"You always have two choices: your commitment versus your fear."* - Sammy Davis, Jr.

If you look at some of the greatest legends of our time, they all have one thing in common – they took a risk. You just heard me say be calculating in your risks, but if you have done that, now it is time to get crackin'! Part of risk-taking is not just physical, but mental, emotional, and spiritual as well. Last year, at 50 years old, I made a complete left turn in a portion of my career. I became the main producer in a $5 million feature film and yet I never have produced a film in my life! Talk about risky. The film business was something I never did before, had little experience with, and the stakes were high. I was not prepared for the energy and the learning curve that came at me. However, I was prepared as a businesswoman, and I applied those skills immediately to this project. I pulled in successful people that know film to help support this opportunity and make it successful. At first, I was clumsy, but I never lost my focus and clarity of what I needed. The support came because I was clear. Knowing that vision with structure is always best when you are creating, but sometimes you just need to roll with it, especially if you want to rock on with your wonderful bad-ass self. Be bold. Don't be afraid to take a risk!

"Fate Loves the Fearless." - James Russell Lowell

Doing anything in life requires balance to do it well. You are not always going to be in perfect union with creating and with change, and that's okay. That is part of nature. However, if you are being bold, fearless and confident, and jumping into the adventure, you will need to recharge your bad-ass self. A lot of stress is created from this place of imbalance, especially here in the United States. We are celebrated for what we do, not for who we are. It is important that if you are going to make a change and really become a bad-ass yourself, you will need to create what I call your "recharge zone." It is a time that you get out of the race for a moment to realign, recharge and refocus your energy. A time for you to tune into your highest potential. In other words, you need to "Seek your Silence." Take some quiet time for you, to clear your thoughts, to hear yourself get out of *doing* and get into the *being* of your life. We live in a world of opposites: light and dark, sun and moon, negative and positive, masculine and feminine. It is important to implement the silence in your life, to counter-balance the high-powered "do" mentality, and all the technology being pushed out at us every single day.

"When you know yourself, you are empowered. When you accept yourself you are invincible." – Tina Lifford

Another important part of succeeding to rock on with your wonderful bad-ass self is accepting you – the good, the bad and the not so pretty. Many times what keeps us from going forward is our need to be perfect. We say to ourselves, "When I have the perfect plan, the perfect career, the right man, the right money, the right education,

I'll move forward with my dream or goal." But sometimes, by waiting for it to be perfect, we never get moving. Or, the opposite happens. We judge ourselves so harshly, and are so critical of ourselves, that we are frozen in time, afraid to get rockin'. We think we are not good enough. We are too fat, too thin. We are too old, too young. The point is, we hold ourselves back in judgment, not ever getting over the fact that the little voice inside of us may not be telling us the truth. If you get into action and stop judging yourself, you may realize that the world is not judging you either. A few years ago when I was a host of a television series, my co-host was about twenty years younger than me. I remember thinking, "I'm old enough to be her mother. I even sort of look like her mother." It was the first time in my career that I became conscious of my age and judging the fact that I was getting older. I also remember wrestling with the voices in my head at the time, saying, "Maybe I am too old to be doing this anymore." All of my critical voices surfaced. These voices created mental images that I call my "perfect pictures." I knew then that for me to go forward in my life, I needed to get to acceptance of myself and look deeper at my worth and what I bring to the table. So, part of you rockin' on with your wonderful bad-ass self is to be more loving and accepting of yourself. I know that I could not be the wonderful bad-ass self I am today without all the things that have brought me to this point, and that includes my age. For a woman in media and entertainment, age is a touchy subject and that is one you have to reconcile with to really ignite your full potential. Now look at your own life. What "perfect pictures" are you carrying around with you? Are you ready to let them go?

> *"Our greatest glory is not in never falling, but in rising every time we fall."* - Confucius

The saying goes, it is not about the fall; it's about the rise. Another part of being a wonderful bad-ass is to know you are going to fall down, and do it anyway. I used to get so scared about failure and rejection. One failure in and I thought it defined me. However, if you talk to the really successful people, failure and rejection are part of getting to your "YES" or success in life.

Failure is part of success. Michael Jordan is a true sports legend, but that doesn't mean he didn't make mistakes or face failure along the way. He was recently quoted as describing his career as a list of failures: "I've missed more than 9000 shots in my career. I've lost almost 300 games. 26 times, I've been trusted to take the game winning shot and missed. I've failed over and over and over again in my life. And that is why I succeed."

Look at J.K. Rowling, author of the mega, best-selling Harry Potter series. Rowling is indisputably one of the most successful writers in the world, yet, she wasn't an overnight success. She spent years in poverty struggling as an undiscovered author and single mother, devoting countless nights in a cafe attempting to make her novel about wizards come to life. She once described herself as "the biggest failure she knew." Her now famous manuscript was rejected 12 times and one publisher even told her to "not to quit her day job." But now, she is the author of the best-selling book series in history, more than 450 million copies worldwide, has won multiple awards and accolades, and the Harry Potter films are the highest-grossing film series in history.

Many people look at famous icons and think they became that way overnight. But you have to remember that even if a person is lucky enough to get that big break, it is not luck that will keep them there. They have to bring the goods, the talent, the integrity, the persistence, and the drive – all of it, in order for it to last. Look at some of the leading women in the media: Oprah Winfrey, Ellen DeGeneres, Hillary Clinton, Arianna Huffington – all of these women have failed at one time or another. The point is, they regrouped and got back up again. It's not the fall that counts. It's having the courage, the strength and the motivation to get back up and try it again! If you are going to be a wonderful bad-ass, you are going to have to get comfortable with both rising and falling. Both of these qualities will make you a true success and give you the ability to make and succeed at change!

> *If you can make a girl laugh, you can make her do anything.*
> *- Marilyn Monroe*

When I was young, I had such a fun energy. However, as I became an adult, I remember thinking, "I have to be responsible," and "It's time to get serious." Part of maturing is doing just that, however, people take it too far. We get stressed out from the small things in life and we stop laughing and having fun. Part of my intention a few years back was to recapture that fun energy I had as a child. I call it, "finding the fun." In doing this you don't have to be doing big things to enjoy yourself. You may find the fun in your everyday life, singing along to the radio while driving in traffic, playing catch with your dog, or just having a gut-wrenching belly laugh with a friend. The point is to not just look for the fun, but to find it and live it in your life – every day. Not just something you do on the weekends or on vacation. I think if you want to be a true, wonderful bad-ass, you need to "Get Your Fun On!" It's too easy to live in stress and take things way too seriously. Just remember that at the end of your life, you are not going to be thinking about your fender-bender from last week or momentary fight with your co-worker. You are going to remember the good times and the meaningful moments with the people around you. So stop, laugh, giggle and let that inner twinkle shine bright. Your homework assignment - HAVE SOME BAD-ASS FUN TODAY!

> *It is the ultimate luxury to combine passion and contribution.*
> *It's also a very clear path to happiness.* - Sheryl Sandberg

I don't know about you, but my life has better meaning and texture to it when I am giving back. Making a contribution to someone else's life, to my community, or to the bigger world can make such a difference. For me, it gives me a sense of connectedness. There are so many people, and you may be one of them, saying, "My life has no purpose." If this is true for you, start making a contribution. Start giving back. By helping someone else, it can instantly give you a sense of purpose, and even passion. Part of rockin' on with your wonderful bad-ass self is knowing that selfless can be better than selfish. By doing some good, and looking for the good, not only are you giving, but I can guarantee that you will be receiving so much in return. If you want to become a better bad-ass, find a way to make a contribution, because you will feel good in the process. The better you feel and the more you help others to change, it can only give you the inspiration to keep making changes yourself.

> *"The more you praise and celebrate your life, the more there is in life to celebrate."* - Oprah Winfrey

How many of you celebrate you? What I mean by that question is, how much time do you spend celebrating all of your wonderful qualities?

Most of us are trained to focus on the negative. You can do 100 things right, but if you do one thing wrong, that will be your focus. We are conditioned in society and in the media to look for the wrong or the negative. Our programming needs to be tweaked in this area. It time to start looking at all the things you are doing right, moving from "wrong" thinking to "right" thinking, and shifting from the negative to the positive. Part of being able to rock on with your wonderful bad-ass self is celebrating and acknowledging your wonderful bad-ass qualities. So this is what I would like you to do:

1. Make a list of five wonderful qualities (list more if you can).

2. Say them out loud.

3. Say them to another person.

4. Say them with passion and conviction.

5. Say them with a bad-ass smile on your face!

Not only do we not get a lot of acknowledgement by the outside world, but we also spend little time, if at all, acknowledging ourselves. In order to be your wonderful bad-ass self, that old conditioning needs to end here and now. It is time to celebrate you! It is truly time to bring forth your good, your magnificence, your power, and your passion! Come on, light your fire!

Let me say that life is not always going to be a breezy ride. You will have your ups and downs, good days and bad. However, if you are committed to making a change and you instill these qualities of fearlessness, vision, structure, action, time, contribution, celebration and fun into your life, you won't just be ready to fulfill your dreams and desires, you will be fully loaded to ROCK ON WITH YOUR WONDERFUL BAD-ASS SELF! - Let's Rock!

To Contact Nina:

Ninainspired2@gmail.com

Telephone 310-798-1699

Websites:

www.lifebites.com

www.rockonwonderful.com

www.goodnightmarilyn.com

Facebook:

www.facebook.com/lifebitestv

www.facebook.com/goodnightmarilyn.com

Twitter: @Lifebites

George Ishee

George Ishee is a recognized expert in the sales and marketing field. With over 28 years of hands on experience, George has trained sales teams with as many as 100% reaching their annual quota 5 years in a row. George has helped hundreds of companies (large and small) develop marketing systems to generate leads on a consistent basis but felt something was still missing.

George has studied both the sales and marketing process throughout his career and was always fascinated at how the mind goes through a decision process and why some people get stuck and some people succeed with ease. There are thousands of books and studies that tell you want is going on and why people do what they do, but there are few tools that people can use to take action. This is what he discovered was missing.

His work with millonairesbygeorge.com is a tool to help anyone break through the limiting beliefs and patterns about money, and is a step by step process to create a new financial future.

A Penny for Your Thoughts

By George Ishee

Has anyone ever asked you if you would like help making your first million dollars? Better yet, have you ever asked yourself, "How can I become a millionaire? What do I need?" What would your answer be? Would you say you need more money, time, knowledge, encouragement, faith, or direction - or perhaps a partner, a drill sergeant, a mentor, or something else? You might require some or all of these resources, but I suggest that the first thing you need is a positive belief system regarding money; one that makes you feel totally convinced in your heart that you would like to be and deserve to be financially free, as well as a roadmap to get there. In this paper, I discuss why I think that is true and provide some practical suggestions for how you can bring about that new way of thinking in your own life.

What do you believe about money?

Many of us simply don't believe that we can - or should - become millionaires because of our past financial conditioning. Think back growing up. Did you often hear such comments as "Money is the root of all evil," "Money doesn't grow on trees," "What, do you think I'm made of money?" or "We can't afford that"? If you did, then you may well have money problems today. Many of our core beliefs - negative and positive - were formed between the ages of 3 and 5 from things we heard from or observed in our parents, and these beliefs are locked in our psyche as adults. As adults, we might want to change some of those negative beliefs, but it's almost impossible to do so without help. The idea that money is a source of worry and the cause of our troubles instead of being a contributor to our happiness is an idea that many of us carry with us on a daily basis. Money should empower you, not hold you back.

How, then, does one change his or her negative beliefs about money and, in doing so, remove this fundamental roadblock to becoming a millionaire? Many successful writers and speakers in the field of personal empowerment have worked to do just that. Perhaps the most famous of these writers, Napoleon Hill, suggests in his book *Think and Grow Rich*, that it is possible to train one's subconscious mind first by creating a positive mental image of what one wants and then visualizing that image over and over in one's conscious mind until the picture is so clear that the subconscious mind accepts it as true. This book, first published in 1937, has sold more than 70 million copies and has no doubt helped many people overcome their self-doubt. Successful motivational speakers and trainers such as Jim Britt, Tom Hopkins, Tony Robbins, and Zig Ziglar, and others, have coached many people to break through subconscious barriers to achieve their dreams and better their lives.

Your mind is in control

And yet, with all this knowledge available in the world, many people still struggle with issues and attitudes about money and the lack of it. Why is that? The answer, I propose, is that these authors and speakers do not control your beliefs about money; you do. And until you deal with your subconscious negative beliefs about money, your financial situation will never change.

To make matters worse, your subconscious does not like you to mess with it, and it has a pretty strong "anti-virus program" that blocks your conscious mind from interfering with the subconscious beliefs. You see, one of the jobs of the subconscious mind is to protect you from potential harm, pain, and discomfort. When it senses these "dangers," it grabs its bag of tools and begins to use them. Some of the most common tools you might recognize are fear, doubt, hesitation, and procrastination, all of which are really just feelings. The problem is that you usually can't identify these feelings easily - often the feelings are so subtle that you don't even notice that they are being used to control your actions, but they do hold you back. The subconscious mind might also use its more powerful tools, such as nervousness and sweating, or even its most formidable tool of all, the fear of death itself, to save us from perceived dangers.

The leash that holds you back

The subconscious hates change and will use any of the tools it has in its arsenal to remain in charge of your actions, make no mistake. The subconscious mind takes the memory of past experiences and events (good or bad) and continually builds a bank of references based on those memories. When you encounter new experiences, it will refer back to this bank of memories, or references. If the references are perceived as painful or harmful, the subconscious mind will block you from taking action. An interesting point is that your subconscious does not care if the experiences are real or not, or whether they are personal memories or memories "borrowed" from others; for the sake of the reference bank, all such memories are accepted as "true." The subconscious mind relies on the reference bank of memories, which it recalls as images, ideas, or series of events ("mental movies") to determine if your actions will be safe or harmful.

The good news is that it's possible to help your subconscious mind retrain itself by replacing some of the negative images stored in your reference bank with more positive ones. This includes replacing your negative views about money with more positive ones that support the notion that you deserve to be wealthy. To do this, you must re-script or "trick" your subconscious by creating a new movie - one that contains images of past successes as well as a clear image of what you want to achieve. Then you must run this movie over and over in your head, with color and sound, until it feels real and becomes the new belief.

Think about how this might work. What if I said to you "Don't think about a big gray elephant, ... don't think about it!" What did you just see in your head? Yes, you saw a big gray elephant, didn't you? How could you do that when I explicitly said NOT to think about it? The reason is that you already have a picture vocabulary in your mind of animals (that is, references in your reference bank) that your subconscious mind refers back to and compares against. Hence, when you read the words "big gray elephant," your mind tapped into your reference bank and called forth the composite of images stored there of what a big gray elephant looks like, and you saw that image instantly.

Get your learner's permit

Now remember the first time you were about to drive a car. Because you had never driven before, you were scared, of course. In fact, you were probably freaking out, and your subconscious mind was pulling out its bag of tools - fear, doubt, hesitation, and apprehension - to keep you from getting behind the wheel and driving. But you decided to press on because you dreamed of the freedom of driving. It didn't take long before getting behind the wheel of a car and driving as no big deal for you.

So how did you create this new pattern of thought? Well, you no doubt did some preparation work first - took a class, obtained your learner's permit, maybe practiced driving around a parking lot with your parents in the car. Nonetheless, the first time you drove out on a road by yourself, I bet it was scary. The second time, it was a bit easier. By the 10th time, you felt fully confident, and your subconscious mind never questioned again your ability to drive because you had provided it with proof that you could drive without wrecking. You replaced the old, negative belief with the new belief that supported your ability to drive. When you get into a car today, do you ever question that can you drive?

Curiosity moves mountains

But how does this apply to finances? I like the story of Kyle McDonald and his adventure with the red paperclip - a humble object that literally changed his life. Every heard of him? Kyle found a red paperclip sitting next to his computer one day and decided to try an experiment. He wanted to see if he could start with a single red paperclip and, by leveraging the value of that paper clip, buy a house. His plan was to barter or trade the paperclip with anybody for something bigger or more valuable - a pen shaped like a fish, a door knob, and even a jet ski. He succeeded in trading the paper clip and, emboldened by his success, kept trading up until he was able to trade for a house that he owned free and clear. He actually achieved this goal in 14 trades, or steps. (You can search the Internet for "one red paperclip" and see exactly how he accomplished it. His story is really quite amazing.)

Kyle was successful because he used his curiosity to create a new belief system. He started small and took baby steps at first. Although he had the ultimate goal of owning a house free and clear, he did not try to trade the paper clip for a house. Instead, he succeeded in small ways at first until he proved to himself that he could do it. Then, when the risks were larger, he had a pattern of success behind him. He believed he could do it, knew he could do it - and he did.

Can you copy Kyle's approach and make it your own? Can you do something similar to help overcome your negative attitudes and beliefs about money? Can you replace your own inner movie with the belief - the certainty - that you can and will become financially free?

Let's explore the idea, but instead of starting with a red paperclip, let's start with a single penny.

Star in your new mental movie

Consider this: When you take a penny and double it 28 times, it equals $1,342,277.20. Isn't that just about how much money you would like in your bank account? If you want, download the document at http://www.millionairesbygeorge.com/images/MBG_Goal_2_YearSchedule.pdf to see the numbers involved in doubling a penny 28 times.

So, all one needs to do is to find a penny and double it 28 times to become a millionaire, right? Well, yes, but…

Immediately, your subconscious kicks in, throwing up roadblocks like, "Wait a minute, I don't have a clue how to double a penny 28 times!" "Nobody has done that before, so it must be impossible - it would be a waste of time!" and so forth. That is your subconscious mind grabbing its powerful tool called skepticism - it's telling you that the concept is silly, or impossible, that you'll look like a fool if you try it, right? That's your old belief system working in full force.

For a moment, ignore that feeling and start to create a new mental movie instead. Imagine, for example, that you see a penny lying on the ground and you pick it up. Take a moment in your mind to consider how it got there. Your subconscious probably told you to ignore it because it wasn't much money, but you went ahead and picked it up anyway. Why?

Suppose you were directed to pick it up? Imagine that a higher power within the universe (something you were not even aware of existed - some would call it the law of attraction) commanded your subconscious to pick it up because that penny had a clear purpose and that purpose was to find you and only you.

Now create a new movie in your head with a script like this: I have been chosen to find that penny, to pick it up, and to use it to lead me to financial success!

To continue with the movie in your heard, take your new penny and double it to two cents. Visualize it. With your skills and talents, could you do that? Of course you could, especially if you financial future was contingent upon it! Then double the two cents to four cents? What about four cents to eight cents? You can probably see how easy it is to keep doubling in these small increments because it's simple. Your subconscious mind agrees and will offer little resistance. In your mind, then, keep doubling the amount; eight to sixteen, sixteen to thirty-two, and so forth, until you get to step 10. Be aware of how easy it is to double a penny 10 times in a row.

Amazingly at step 10 you'll only have reached $5.12. Are you surprised at the small amount? Within those 10 steps, however, you have silently been building a new repetitive script that your subconscious mind sees and is certainly not threatened by - the repetition has simply confirmed the fact you can double successfully. This is how you trick your subconscious. It takes about 10 successful repetitions to create in your mind the "proof" that this action is comfortable and non-threatening; your mind stores this information as a new reference in your memory bank. This is your new "mental movie;" in essence, you have supplied your subconscious mind with a new positive belief about money.

From this point on (around step 10), something magical happens. Your subconscious mind will now accept that you can, in fact, double your money because you have just done it 10 times in a row. Instead of questioning whether you can double your money to the next step, it will now focus on asking the question "how can I double it?" This is a major mental breakthrough.

Secrets to success: Just do it

Now, you only need one more tool, which is the knowledge of how to double your money at each step, to make a financial breakthrough. Once you know the answer of how to do it, all the pieces come together.

You can gain the knowledge either on your own by trial and error, or you can learn from the example others who have already done it before you. That is, you can learn what they did and simply copy it.

If, for example, you asked me how you can double your money from $5.12 (step 10) to $10.24 (step 11), I would recommend that you do what someone I know did—go to a yard sale this weekend and find something that you know you could sell for $10.24 and offer them $5.12. Could you do that? It might require you making multiple offers or visiting multiple yards sales, but do you see yourself doubling your money from $5 to $10 in this way?

And herein lies a little secret. You already know from attending yard sales or flea markets that anything can be sold for less than market value and resold for a higher price. It happens all the time—as the saying goes, "one man's junk is another man's treasure." So, become the expert on what things are worth; that is, on what people are willing to pay for something. Then find someone that no longer needs that item and purchase it from them for a lower price and sell it for a higher price. Haven't you ever sold anything for less than market value yourself and were happy to get rid of it? Once you start learning the true monetary value of things, it's easy to find people who are willing and able to sell things to you at a lower price than the true market value. Isn't this what every current millionaire has done to become a millionaire… Buy low and sell high and make a profit?

Is it hard to learn to buy low and sell high? Of course not, if you know the market value of items. Some familiar resources, such as ebay.com, craigslist.org, amazon.com, and the classified ads in your local newspaper, can help you determine the market value of items for free. When you master the skill of finding a good deal, buying low and selling high can be duplicated at each of the 28 steps. Just use the same process with higher priced items.

The proof is in the penny

It's funny, when I share this concept of doubling a penny to becoming a millionaire, the most common reaction I hear is, "Yes it is easy to double a penny in small increments, but when you get to the big numbers, it must be really difficult, so why try?" Are you thinking the same thing? I laugh because I know that I am hearing people's subconscious fears talking to me!

Here is the key: once your subconscious mind has the proof it needs, you will never have that thought again. Don't believe me? Prove it to yourself. Go ahead; create a new movie in your head. Visualize the process you would follow to double a penny in 10 steps. Then go out and find a penny in the next week and double it to $5.12 in 90 days and see if I am right!

I've brought up this idea of doubling a penny to reach financial freedom with a lot of friends over the past 2 years and they finally pestered me enough to take action and to create a Web site that they could use as their personal roadmap to double their pennies and become a millionaire. So I created *Millionaires by George*. The site is intended to provide both a roadmap and online journal that anyone can use to track their 28-step journey to becoming a millionaire. If one signs up as a member on the site, you also gain access to an online community of others who are making their own way through the 28 steps to becoming a millionaire. With each step, the site provides (in advance) the knowledge of how all the other members have completed the step you are about to start. Once you complete a step, you are asked to share your answer with the other members who are at an earlier step, and you let those ahead of you tell you what to do next. It's a "pay it forward" concept. If you like the idea, visit www.millionairesbygeorge.com or email us your questions or comments to support@millionairesbygeorge.com

Go ahead, take my challenge and start looking for a penny and see how fast you find it because that penny is already looking for you! Be curious, and try doubling it 10 times in 90 days or less and watch how quickly your belief about money changes. Remember, all it takes is a penny to change your thoughts!

Contact: George Ishee – support@millionairesbygeorge.com

Jennifer S. Wilkov

Jennifer S. Wilkov is a #1 international best-selling award-winning author, an award-winning freelance writer, a media personality and executive producer, the Literary Agent Matchmaker™ and a respected book & business consultant in her business called "Your Book Is Your Hook!" She is also a blogger for books for the Huffington Post, and a columnist for the award-winning magazine PUBLISHED and Book Marketing Magazine. She supports first time writers and seasoned authors with the essentials to become a bestseller: a great project, a strong platform and a well-polished pitch, presentation and hook for their book. She educates and assists them with the writing, marketing and getting published processes (traditional with an agent, self-publishing and e-publishing) for their book ideas and projects as well as the building of their platform to raise their visibility to readers, the media, Hollywood and beyond. She also guides them with the steps to take their creative ideas to Hollywood film and television as well as Broadway theater. She continues to passionately teach and educate writers as a speaker at writers' conferences and for groups and teaches online for writers' resources such as The Writers Store, Writers Digest, and others. She also produces The Next Bestseller™ Weekend Workshop that provides exclusive access to industry professionals for 15 fortunate writers each year.

Books: A Life-Changing Experience for Reader & Writer Alike

By Jennifer S. Wilkov

Books change lives. It's a fact. Once you have read a book, whether it is fiction, nonfiction or a children's book, it changes you in some way. Maybe it makes you smile or laugh. Maybe it haunts you. Maybe it educates you and, as a result of reading it, you learned something you didn't know before. Books cultivate change for people young and old. It's a fact.

From way, way back, many centuries ago, stories and the telling of them has not only kept our cultures alive, they have helped to shape them and the people in every community. We talk about how our ancestors shared stories to keep tales of the Bible alive, tales of historical events alive, tales of heroes and villains alive, and tales that teach morals, skills and philosophies so they can pass from one person to the next and generation to generation.

Fast forward from the days when storytellers were respected members of tribes and ethnic groups to more modern day stories such as those that changed us as children. Dr. Seuss and his books come to mind, changing us in ways through fun, quick, short books that are memorable. Who can forget about *Horton Hears a Who, The Lorax, Oh The Places You'll Go,* and the other precious books he wrote? We grew up on them, just like we did Beatrix Potter's collection of stories about Peter Rabbit and his friends and Winnie the Pooh and

The House at Pooh Corner written by A.A. Milne. The lessons, joys, sorrows, and fun we had reading these books may still bring a smile to your face as I mention them here. They stayed with us. They changed us as children. They helped us grow and evolve. There are many books published to fulfill our changing appetites as we grow up. Books are a beacon for many of us – an indication of the changing tides in our lives.

The length of a book doesn't matter when it comes to the impact it has on us and our lives. *Les Miserables* by Victor Hugo, a book about change itself and the French Revolution, was 1,488 pages. *Who Moved My Cheese* by Spencer Johnson, M.D., on the other hand, was just 96 short pages. It is what is inside them that matters and that changes us.

When we are cultivating change in our own lives, we turn to books that have been fashioned in such a way so we can use them as a resource and guide, to the changes we would like to make. For example, books such as Rick Warren's *The Purpose Driven Life* or James Redfield's *The Celestine Prophecy* help us to reformulate the way we see and interact with our world.

WHY WRITING A BOOK CHANGES LIVES – BOTH THE LIVES OF THE READERS AND THE WRITERS

People who choose to write books face an enormous reality that when they are finished, the book they have written will have also changed them in addition to those who read their work.

Examples of books you may know that didn't just change our lives but the life of the writer include *The Joy of Cooking* by Irma S. Rombauer. This book is often a staple in our lives today, both at home and in commercial kitchens, but for Irma, it literally saved her life. You see, Irma, who was a homemaker, privately published this book originally in 1931 in St. Louis, Missouri, following her husband's suicide the previous year. She was struggling emotionally and financially. She had 3,000 copies of her book printed by a company which had printed labels for fancy St. Louis shoe companies and for Listerine®, but never a book. In 1936, the book was picked up by a commercial printing house and the rest was history. It has been in print continuously since then and sold more than 18 million copies. Irma's book didn't just change everyone's life that bought it; it changed her life and her family's lives forever.

J.K. Rowling lived a "rags to riches" story of her own with the *Harry Potter* book series she wrote. Rowling was working as a secretary and researcher for Amnesty International when she conceived the idea for the *Harry Potter* series on a delayed train trip from Manchester to London in 1990. The seven years that followed included the death of her mother, a divorce from her first husband, and relative poverty. Seven years after graduating from university, Rowling saw herself as a failure. Her marriage had failed, and she was jobless with a dependent child. She was diagnosed at that time with depression and even contemplated suicide. Rowling signed up for welfare benefits, describing her economic status as being "poor as it is possible to be in modern Britain, without being homeless." Rowling went on to finish her manuscript on an old manual typewriter in 1997. When Bloomsbury, a publishing house in London, agreed to publish the book, her editor advised Rowling to get a day job, since she had little chance of making money in children's books. Rowling's books indeed changed her life just as much as they changed the lives of so many children and families worldwide. She progressed from living on state benefits to multi-millionaire status within five years. Her books have won multiple awards and sold more than 400 million copies. Talk about changing lives!

Books and the ways they are written have changed over the years just as much as the writers who write them. Books were written mostly by individuals. There was not much to it. Simply take out your trusty typewriter and let your imagination run wild.

Then, in 1937, Napoleon Hill wrote one of the earliest motivational personal development and self-help books as a result of an inspiration suggested by businessman Andrew Carnegie. *Think and Grow Rich* was written by Hill with the intention that the philosophy taught in the book could be used to help people succeed in all lines of work and to do or be almost anything they want. The book was first published during the Great Depression. Hill had actually conducted 20 years of research based on his close association with individuals who achieved great wealth during their lifetimes. He studied the characteristics of these achievers to develop laws of success and form a philosophy of personal achievement. He then coalesced this into the book many of us have read. At the time of his death in 1970, more than 20 million copies had been sold. By 2011, more than 70 million copies had been sold worldwide.

Books continue to change lives, even after the writer is dead. The books live on and so does their impact on the human race. Whether it is Irma Rombauer's *The Joy of Cooking*, Napoleon Hill's *Think and Grow Rich*, or Dr. Seuss's books, the truth is the writers may not be with us, but the books they wrote still are.

Today, books are still written by individual writers or writing partners. Other books are coalesced from interviews and studies like Napoleon Hill's book. Book content or chapters are also solicited by individuals who curate a multiple co-author type of book, like the one you are reading now, and publish it as the "provocateur" of the material as opposed to being the "author" of the book.

WHY BOOKS WILL CONTINUE TO CULTIVATE CHANGE

Some books have actually become phenomena themselves, set records, and changed lives in their wake. The *Chicken Soup for the*

Books: A Life-Changing Experience for Reader & Writer Alike

Soul® books came on the scene in 1993 with the idea that people could help each other by sharing the stories about their lives. The best 101 stories were compiled in the first book. Today, more than 250 books have been published in a variety of categories from teenagers to breast cancer to pets to the military and more. These books are not only changing the lives of the writers, who have all become bestsellers, they are changing the millions of lives of the readers by sharing the stories of many people in each book.

Books like *Fifty Shades of Grey* by British author E.L. James, an erotic romance novel published in 2011 that took the worldwide market by storm and brought elements of sexual practices to the forefront for readers, have also created change and phenomena. The book also changed its course for publishing, originally starting out as a self-published electronic book also available through print-on-demand publishing. It got picked up by Vintage Books in 2012 and became a best-selling book and the series sold over 100 million copies worldwide in 52 different languages.

Books have not only changed people, but industries too. In fact, adaptations of books have appeared in the Academy Award categories since the second annual presentation of the Oscar Awards. They have appeared in the Guinness Book of World Records since 1954, after it was first conceived in 1951 by the then managing director of Guinness Breweries. Ironically, the book itself holds a world record, as one of the best-selling copyrighted books of all time. It is also one of the most frequently stolen books from public libraries in the United States.

HOW TO CULTIVATE CHANGE WITH YOUR BOOK

For some, they will never write their books. For others, they struggle with writing them, thus the book project itself becomes a catalyst for change. It provides the opportunity for the writer him or herself to change.

Writing and publishing a book is not predicated on whether you can actually write. You can enlist resources to help you write, market, and publish your book idea. It is often said that the book chooses the writer, as opposed to the writer choosing the book idea. When you say, "Someone should write a book about that!" Guess what? That is why you are the one who should write it since you understand the change and difference a book like that would make for others. You will therefore write it differently than someone who doesn't understand the value the book brings to the lives of others.

As a writer, you may become a leader in your field, community or organization. You may be revered by readers who clamor for more of your stories. Authors such as Shel Silverstein, Maya Angelou, Mitch Albom, John Grisham, E.L. Doctorow, Ursula Le Guin, and many others have risen to recognition for their writing and, as a result, changed the landscape, paradigms, and motivations of many.

The truth is that many may have a book idea, but it is a small percentage of people who ever write and publish their books. These are the change makers. They are courageous and willing to finish their book projects. They contribute to their community and, inherently, contribute to the Greater Good. Charles Dickens, as an example, in his day wanted to express the social conscience he saw that was missing. In the society he lived in, he spoke of responsibility and ideas for how one individual could be a good citizen within the community that they lived. After all, he was the one who said, "It was the best of times, it was the worst of times."

Take a look at this brief list of leaders from various walks of life, as they have all taken the time to write a book and change lives as a result: Richard Branson, Donald Trump, His Holiness The Dalai Lama, Martha Stewart, Jack Welch, Carly Fiorina, L. Ron Hubbard, Dr. Mehmet Oz, Lou Holtz, and more. The list goes on and on of leaders who have books. The difference between you and them is that they get more gigs, are noticed by the media, and have more opportunities to cultivate change than you do if you don't have a book.

Even politicians these days use books as part of their own marketing campaigns and messaging strategies to cultivate change and swing voters. Our own President Obama used his books to inform the American public about who he is, where he came from and what he believes when he ran for office.

Every writer begins experiencing the changes a book project and writing can bring to their lives in the same humble ways. They start at the beginning, with nothing - no bestsellers, no following or fans, and no publisher. They change as a result of their writing experiences, and thereby cultivate change in others who are grateful for their courage to write.

One of America's most wildly popular and beloved women's fiction authors began the same way, with nothing, and an even bigger challenge. Debbie Macomber is dyslexic and didn't learn to read until she was in the fifth grade. Her dyslexia did not deter the young mother of four from pursuing a lifelong dream of becoming published. Debbie didn't get a book published during her first five years as a writer. Today, with more than 130 million copies of her books in print, Debbie Macomber is one of the world's most popular best-selling authors. Not bad for a woman who is dyslexic and didn't learn to read until she was in the fifth grade.

Nicholas Sparks is another well-known writer who charted an unexpected course of changing his own life and, as a result, the lives of others with his books. After receiving a full track scholarship to the University of Notre Dame, he got injured during his freshman year in college after breaking the Notre Dame record in the 4 x 800 relay. He spent the summer icing his Achilles tendon and moping around the house until his mother said, "Don't just pout, do something." When Nicholas, sulking, asked "What?" – his mother replied, "I don't know. Write a book." He looked at her and said, "Okay."

The first novel he wrote eight weeks later was never published. His second novel in 1989, was also never published. It is kept together with countless rejection slips, alongside his first novel. He decided to concentrate on another career. In addition to being rejected from law school, Nicholas appraised real estate, bought and restored houses, waited tables, sold dental products by phone and finally started his own business (manufacturing orthopedic products).

During this time, he wrote yet another book, *Wokini*, with Billy Mills, a long-time friend and Olympic Gold Medalist that was published by a small publisher. It did well regionally and was picked up by Random House in 1994. The success, Sparks confesses, was primarily due to the name recognition of Billy Mills.

In early 1992, he sold his business and looked around for something to do. He became a pharmaceutical salesman. In May 1994, he decided to give writing another shot. He wrote *The Notebook* over a six-month period. In July 1995, he started soliciting agents. He found one and the book was presented to publishers in October 1995. At the time, he was earning about $40,000 a year. Warner Books bought the rights for $1,000,000. Film rights to the novel were sold later that same week to New Line Cinema and foreign rights were sold (eventually into more than 45 languages). Now that's a big change!

Finally, let's look at the humble beginnings of Dan Brown, a New Hampshire native, who taught English and creative writing at Phillips Exeter Academy until 1998, when he became a full time writer and his first novel, *Digital Fortress,* was published. That first book was followed by *Angels and Demons* in 2001, and *Deception Point* in 2002.

But it wasn't until his fourth novel that Dan Brown's career as a

Books: A Life-Changing Experience for Reader & Writer Alike

writer and best-selling author took off. In fact, his first three novels were virtually unknown until he broke out with the runaway hit, *The Da Vinci Code,* that went on to sell more than 25 million copies in 44 languages and was made into a feature film starring Tom Hanks. *Time* magazine in its 2005 article, "The Novel That Ate the World," stated that during the two years prior to its article, one of the very few books to sell more copies than *The Da Vinci Code* was the Bible.

The truth is that Dan Brown's life was changed ironically by another writer, Sidney Sheldon. Brown resolved to become a writer when he read Sidney Sheldon's *The Doomsday Conspiracy* while vacationing in Tahiti. After reading Sheldon's book, which he found swift and merciless, he began to suspect that maybe he could write a 'thriller' of this type one day. He'd read almost no commercial fiction at all since the Hardy Boys as a child. After his first two novels, his sales were poor and by 2001 he was in the same rut as so many authors - handling his own publicity and even selling books out of his car, a process that would now require a convoy of trucks.

Brown changed agents, changed publishers (from Simon & Schuster to Doubleday, a Random House imprint), changed his luck, and then – he changed the industry.

He wrote the outline for *The Da Vinci Code* in a laundry room, himself planted in a lawn chair and his manuscript balanced on an ironing board. It was published in March 2003, and was an immediate hit that remained on bestseller lists for more than three years.

The amount of change you can impact in our world is endless when you choose to write your book. Imagine if Debbie let the dyslexia beat her, or if Nicholas gave up after he got nothing but rejection slips for his second novel, or if Dan Brown decided to stop writing after his first two novels weren't selling well. If he hadn't sat down in that laundry room and written *The Da Vinci Code*, well, the history of the book publishing industry just wouldn't be the same, now would it?

I really do believe that your book is your hook. Books cultivate change in our world.

As a writer, and a maker of change, consider how you can best make your teachings and ideas accessible to others. Choose wisely and write purposefully.

We will all reap the rewards for many years to come – and so will you.

But one fact remains: you can't use your book as your hook and change lives with it – until you have a book.

To Contact Jennifer:

www.YourBookIsYourHook.com

www.TheNextBestseller.com

www.LinkedIn.com/in/JenniferWilkov

www.Twitter.com/JenniferWilkov

www.Facebook.com/YourBookIsYourHook

Harry Kroner

Harry Kroner is the founder of *Life Achieved* and creator of cutting edge healing programs such as *Freedom From Anxiety*, *Deep Personal Healing*, and *Emotional Wisdom & Self Mastery*. He brings a unique blend of deep healing to all levels of your being: body, heart, mind, and soul. He has become a leading expert in soul healing and deep emotional healing.

He is a graduate of the University of Massachusetts in Psychology, and received extensive training in hypnotherapy, energy psychology, life coaching, NLP, energy healing, and Quantum Healing Hypnosis Therapy.

Harry has helped thousands of individuals reach a happier, balanced, and wiser version of themselves. Helping many bring peace into their lives in his office, around the country and the world, through phone and Skype sessions. He conducts workshops and seminars to groups, bringing his teachings, healing processes, personal growth and insight to many more. He is also the author of the upcoming book *Emotional Wisdom*.

Deep Healing

By Harry Kroner

"Healing does not mean the damage never existed, it means the damage no longer controls our lives." - Unknown.

Our hearts and souls are truly the core of who we are. All deep healing needs to first of all take place in these core levels in order to bring a lasting change for our entire being. Nothing resonates stronger than tangible stories of true healing and the potential of all that is possible. Here are two stories of healing my clients experienced. I hold these close to my heart, and would like to share them with you.

Alice came to my office following some devastating news her doctors gave her. It surprised me when she said that although she is in her early thirties, she is experiencing post-menopausal hormonal levels, and basically her ovaries have shut down completely and resembled that of an elderly woman, with no turning back. The doctors told her she will not be able to have any children! This news destroyed her. She was a professional woman who chose to wait to have children until she meets the right partner; and now the news that she will not be able to have any shattered her to the core.

I knew intuitively that we needed to work on the underlying spiritual cause of this. She was a healthy, vibrant woman, fully intent on healing and very open to spiritual work. There was a lot to accomplish and we spent several sessions healing and releasing the shock, anger, and other negative emotions surrounding her new condition.

We went deeper to explore past lives and discovered that she had a baby in one of her early incarnations as a young mother. She had lost her child in that life and her grief was palpable to me through time and space, as the tears rolled down Alice's face. After calming her down and bringing her to a more comfortable place, more unraveled. Insight and wisdom was flowing through her easily. She was conveying to me that none of her following lives had any children in them because of the terrible trauma incurred in the early life. The following lives have been shifted because of it, altering the life plans and purposes, as the soul could not bear experiencing it again.

Much was released; and with my help, she let go of the trauma from that first life. And through conversing with her guides, she understood that she still has a choice whether she would like to have children or not in this lifetime. This gave her much to think about, as she was not completely clear whether she did want children or not. We decided to go even deeper and employ the Quantum Healing Hypnosis Therapy method. I knew this method will connect us directly to her soul and heal anything in the body that needed healing, if this was truly in her destiny and free will choice.

The session was amazing and we cleared other significant issues that she was dealing with in her life, and more light was shed on the matter. Alice was given the true core issue of why the medical condition suddenly appeared. Her body was answering the commands of her soul to shut down all reproductive systems, because Alice started developing a significant relationship with a wonderful man and that scared her soul to the core. It was putting all the stops in her body to prevent her from conceiving a baby in this life, so the pain and suffering of losing another baby will not be repeated. This shocked Alice slightly even though it all started to make sense. She concluded she wanted to have the option of having children, even if she is not sure about it at the moment.

We asked for complete healing of the ovaries and her reproductive system so they may resume their normal functioning as well as other health and emotional areas that needed attention. During the experience, Alice was mentioning how she could feel light and healing happening in this area of her body. We received deep revelations about her life's blueprint and purpose in this session - a lot of explanation of the spiritual reasons behind certain events in her lifetime that brought much pain. She was blown away with the material and wisdom that was transpiring.

The results came through a week later at her next test. The doctors were amazed. They could not explain it, but the ovaries resumed complete normal functioning. The hormone levels that were extremely low, had increased back to normal range. I was thrilled - another happy resolution and great healing of body, mind and soul.

But we were not done. She was not clear within herself whether she wanted children or not. Much doubt, deep fear, and indecisiveness brought the medical issues back, and by her next routine checkup, the problem returned.

At this point, we both knew that she is causing this to herself on the deepest levels, just as most of us cause our physical ailments to ourselves for some reason or another, we all do! This is not a conscious choice, but one that comes from much deeper within the subconscious mind, heart, and soul. Rooted in emotional trauma both from this life and others.

We went back to work, and this time I was going global, or more precisely - universal. And I was releasing all blocks and fears from her subconscious and soul level as high as we could reach. Asking her guides and higher self to clear all remaining blocks and fears

The Change 3

from the soul level down through the heart, mind and the body. Releasing ALL karmic issues revolving this subject from all past and future lifetimes, allowing her to experience motherhood if she so wishes.

Alice described to me that she was experiencing a circle of loving beings around her, with much healing light and energy flowing through her, and they were writing down in their notebooks, as if correcting things in her life's blueprint and re-writing her history and future.

These were profound sessions. She was allowing and creating great healing on herself from all levels of her being. Now, it was about believing and allowing; we worked on that as well, internalizing and integrating our work to her consciousness. It felt certain and complete. I got the intuition that it was done!

Three months had gone by and I opened an email from Alice that started with "WOW, you wouldn't believe this, but I'm pregnant!" I was so excited. She calculated and realized that her partner and she conceived only days after our last session. She wanted to meet again in order to give the whole pregnancy and child a shield of protection, making sure everything will go smoothly. During the session in the altered state, she saw her guides and other helpers spinning around her creating layers of light. We also spoke to the soul of the unborn child along with her guides to see what else can be done to make sure this pregnancy will be a success, and making sure it will be done.

At the end of the session, she told me that her fertility doctor is one of the most prominent doctors in the field, and that in his forty years of practicing, he had seen only a handful of cases where this "spontaneous healing" occurred. She smiled to herself and decided not to tell him about all of our work, as she sensed that he simply would not understand, or believe it anyway.

Deep Healing

Time has gone by and she came into my thoughts once again. I sent her an email inquiring how is she doing. I opened her reply email and saw a beautiful picture of her grinning face, holding a healthy baby boy!

I have witnessed this level of deep healing many times in my practice. I know and believe through pure fact and results, that we all hold great powers of healing. We can heal practically anything. Not everyone is open enough to see and believe this is possible, but it is. We just need to know how to tap into this, believe in our power, understand the deeper spiritual purpose, gain wisdom, wider perspective, then release and heal our body, mind, heart and soul - gaining the freedom to become all that we truly are, to experience this lifetime's journey to its full potential and grow.

It is important to know that not everyone is ready to go so deeply to our source and heal from the highest level. However, it does not mean that significant and deep healing cannot be attained. Much of our pain and challenges lie in the heart and subconscious mind and can be resolved in other ways. Most of our issues do come from triggers and experiences of this life. When we combine these with certain tendencies we inherit in our DNA, it could manifest into serious levels if left untreated.

Some issues scream at us so loudly that we show many obvious symptoms to ourselves and our environment, pressing us for a quick resolution, or at least relief from the unrelenting symptoms. In many cases the need for relief from those symptoms becomes the main focus in modern medicine, and addressing the deeper core issues is simply left untreated. These continue to fester and cause even more issues and manifestation in the body, as it begs for resolution. Most people stop at this level, and avoid or simply do not know that deeper healing can be reached - completely releasing them from this unnecessary cycle of suffering.

The Change 3

Dennis suffered from severe generalized anxiety. He was brought to my office with the assistance of a family member, otherwise he would not have come, as he was petrified of going to new places and meeting new people. He was shaking slightly with a heightened level anxiety. I went out of my way to make him feel comfortable. Most people do not comprehend how devastating anxieties can be to the people who suffer from them.

He did not feel safe leaving his home. He stopped working and was very anxious going anywhere. He was in a constant state of high anxiety, experiencing a relentless barrage of negative thoughts that never left him. He was on medication but knew he wanted to resolve the deeper issues under the surface. He just could not continue living in this hell. He was at his wits' end.

Dennis is tall and wide, but you could see he was only a shadow of his former self - looking smaller and feeling smaller than he really is. Constant fear ruled his life. He only spoke of his level of anxieties - constantly assessing his well-being based on how bad the anxiety was today, or this week. His coping mechanisms were doing everything to avoid any trigger, event, or situation that might bring a panic attack; which are exceptionally unpleasant and bring a sense of total loss of control. The fear of an anxiety attack became his greatest anxiety, a hostage within his own body, as fear and avoidance completely took over.

We worked together for a while, slowly but surely building trust, creating a deeper sense of safety, and giving him many tools to reduce the anxiety. This produced mild results and progress. I felt it my mission to help him get better and really go for deeper healing with him. A concept for an entire program popped into my mind: "Freedom from Anxiety," and I wrote down everything that worked for him and others I helped with anxieties. I thought to myself, if I can help Dennis reclaim his life, healing his severe manifestation of anxiety, I could help scores of other people who suffer from this debilitating and very common tendency.

I started applying many different techniques and tools to help him on his journey of healing. He was relaxing deeper and deeper with every session. We applied many techniques to re-pattern his thought processes from his subconscious, neutralizing many of the triggers. We did an exploration of root causes in his heart and mind and cleared many of them. He responded beautifully to energy healing techniques that we did in my office and some he could do at home. These brought the most significant change for him.

It got clearer and clearer that he lived too much in his head and he completely blocked his heart, building a wall around it to protect it from any anxiety and fear. Unfortunately this is the state of many people in the western world - building elaborate guards and walls around our hearts, in the erroneous attempt of not getting hurt; trying to stifle emotional pain and fear, thinking that suppressing it will bring relief. The real solution is making peace with our emotions, understanding what they are here to teach us; and then those emotions simply dissipate and release naturally and fully. We are constantly encouraged to make rational decisions while ignoring our emotions, repressing them, without truly healing them.

Dennis started opening his heart center, and allowed wellness to flow through it once again. He started coming into my office with more confidence and greater presence; speaking more freely. And his constant assessment of the anxiety became insignificant. He wanted to do more than just treat his anxiety, and we started working on healthier lifestyle and eating habits. He still had some social anxieties, but he was slowly conquering them one by one. He was able to go grocery shopping again and go for walks around the neighborhood without experiencing high anxiety. He applied for a new job and started working gradually. Dennis was reclaiming his life.

The Change 3

He seemed to be doing better and better. We had reached the point when he told me he felt he didn't need to come and see me anymore. I felt so deeply moved by his progress in those few short months. I knew I was ready to help more people with similar tendencies. Seemingly out of the blue, I received numerous new requests for help with anxieties. Many common threads of this tendency for anxiety glared me in the face. Yet, I was constantly admiring the uniqueness of each individual and their own manifestations and deeper subconscious reasons of why these anxieties flared up. Seeing the relief in people's eyes when the anxieties no longer hold power over them is exceptionally rewarding for me.

We all have something that needs healing. Even if it lies deeper inside and we don't feel like it is interfering with our normal functioning, it still does. Just because we got used to carrying our baggage with us does not mean it is not heavy, or that we will not feel a lot lighter and happier after we have healed.

The point is not to simply rid yourself of negativity, it is the insight and wisdom upon your inner works. It is a peace process that must take place within each and every one. It is time to end internal conflict and bring peace and wellness to your life. I call it emotional wisdom: the deep process of learning the deep lesson from our experiences and emotions but from a place of curiosity, courage, and kindness to yourself.

The cost of not addressing your issues and internal conflict is greater than you think. The suffering we hold on to by not healing brings us dis-ease of the body, mind, and heart. By leaving things as they are, you sentence yourself to endless suffering and misery on varying degrees. Deep healing is freeing yourself to be all that you truly are. As the quote in the beginning clearly says, it is more about regaining our power over our lives... not allowing events, people, or tendencies to rule us in any way. You are more powerful than you think.

It is a self-created illusion that things, triggers, other people, have power over us. That you are a victim, a passenger in your own life witnessing how other powers pull you and you have no control. It is an illusion. There is no damage that cannot be deeply healed. You are a powerful being with enormous power of healing that stems from an endless source of love. It is within you. You can grasp it, and there is plenty of help available to you. You just need to ask. Just know it is possible. You deserve to be balanced, happy, and free.

Contact me:

Harry Kroner

harry@lifeachieved.com

www.LifeAchieved.com

www.OrionsGateway.com

(508) 709-0907

Julie Anne Christoph, CPC, ELI-MP

Founder Canadian Coaching Academy

Director, iPEC Canada

Julie Anne Christoph's bold determination, practical wisdom, and conscious style of living led her from a series of spirit-killing jobs to her life's dream of helping people connect with their true selves. She turned a passion for exercise into owning a Curves women's fitness center where she discovered her talent for coaching people. Her leadership at Curves led to a challenging role as Area Director for Curves International. In 2010, Julie Anne followed her heart and became a Certified Professional Coach (CPC) through iPEC's Accredited Coach Training Program. She was so passionate about her coaching experience that she founded the Canadian Coaching Academy to certify iPEC coaches in Canada, where she has been training and inspiring coaches ever since.

She also cofounded ConsciousChanges.com to give people the tools to live a conscious and authentic life – tools such as The Change Revolution Program to discover your true self and the Start Out Steps (SOS) Program that provides entrepreneurs with practical knowledge to build a successful business consciously. Through speaking engagements, workshops, conferences and programs, Julie Anne helps entrepreneurs create the outcomes they desire, personally and professionally, by championing inner reflection, personal empowerment, conscious choices and living true to oneself every day.

Conscious Change For A Happy Life

By Julie Anne Christoph

There are very few people who live their lives by design. We have the best of intentions, but change is hard and we seem to always fall back into familiar patterns. To change our lives and live a truly conscious life, we must change our results:

- to change our results we must change our actions;

- to change our actions, we must change how we feel; and,

- to change how we feel we must change our thinking.

> *"We are what we think. All that we are arises with our thoughts. With our thoughts we make the world."*
>
> - Hindu Prince Gautama Siddhartha, the founder of Buddhism, 563-483 B.C.

We live in a fast-paced society that has been imposed on us and live life on the run: get to work, hurry home, cook dinner, do laundry, get the kids to activities, etc. Text messages, emails, and phone calls come in at a furious pace. We are impatient, pre-occupied and busy and we hate our jobs, but stay because it puts food on the table and a roof over our heads.

We have lost touch with our families, our friends and ourselves. We don't really know how to connect with each other anymore and we don't take the time to think. The stress is relentless and damaging.

In 2002, I took responsibility for my life. I experienced a total burn-out and stopped working for five months. I was so disconnected from myself that I would wake up at night to hate my boss, blaming him for the state I was in.

I remember one day saying to myself that all this had to stop. I wanted to get back on my feet and I was the only one who had the power to do it. So I started asking myself deep questions like:

- What do I *truly* want?

- Who am I *really*?

- What is *really* important to me?

- What do *I* love?

To my surprise, I did not have the answers to these questions. This led me on a journey of self-discovery or, as I love to say, a safari - it sounds more fun!

I began to realize that we are raised as robots on an assembly line. At school they teach us in a certain way because it's easier for the teacher. They impose beliefs (consciously or not) about who we are and what we're capable of. Beliefs like: "Women don't make it to the top," "If you want people to like you, you have to compromise," and "If you don't go to university, you'll never be successful," are entrenched in our society. We make these beliefs our own and shape our lives around them, limiting ourselves right from the start. Our subconscious mind runs the show and we are on autopilot.

BUT WAIT! It doesn't have to be that way. You can create conscious change and choose to build an authentic and happy life that's right for you.

So if you want to start a revolution in your life, take the time to STOP AND BREATHE... and keep reading!

***

Everyone is capable of living a conscious life. Nowadays, we hear it from everywhere - what we must do to be more fulfilled and happier - but we're afraid to take the steps to get there. Susan, a talented photographer and entrepreneur, was part of a coaching group for my Change Revolution Program. Susan was unhappy in her relationship with her husband and wanted more. Her home-based photography business had plateaued, and although she still had great passion for photography, she had lost her passion for running her business.

Susan was confused and needed clarity – she had lost sight of herself and wasn't sure who she was, what she wanted, and how to go about creating change in her life.

Through the value exercise and alignment segment of The Change Revolution Program, Susan began to reconnect with herself and she set herself a challenge: to spend one-on-one time with her husband, something that was rare. On their first date night, Susan had a plan to connect at a deeper level with her partner. To her great surprise, her husband avoided every attempt at serious conversation about their relationship. It was her big aha moment!

Everything became clear to Susan. Knowing who she was and what she wanted, she took charge of her life, stepped into her power and left the relationship. It was a difficult choice to strike out on her own with two young kids and relocate her photography studio, but she knew it was the right move for her.

Since then, everything has changed for her. She bought a house on her own and has a much happier life with her children. She opened a retail photography studio and has 18 people working with her, tripling her business from $85,000 to $235,000 in a year and a half. Susan is now able to communicate her needs with the people in her life. She was in a relationship for a year but ended it because it wasn't aligned with her values and goals (thanks to work done with the Change Revolution Program).

Susan made a conscious choice versus a fear-based choice. When a choice is based on fear, we convince ourselves that it is the "right choice" because the feared outcome seems real. A conscious choice puts you in a position of power because you take the time to assess what you truly want and question its impact holistically – the effect your choice has on every aspect of your life: career, family life, intimacy, social life, your mental state – everything that your choice has an influence on. Only then are you able to see clearly if the choice is in alignment with your beliefs and how you want to live your life.

Susan is super grateful to have created her Change Revolution – she's taking care of herself and has found happiness and peace in her life. It's incredible how you can manifest what you truly want when you face your fears and become clear about who you really are!

***

When we struggle in our lives, we tend to look around us and compare ourselves to others, which usually makes the situation worse. Going inward, to determine what we really want, is the only way to find our way.

Heather was a graduate of my iPEC Canada Accredited Coaching Program and I saw her again at her group's reunion. As everyone shared what was happening in their lives since the course ended, Heather told us that she wasn't experiencing any of the success the others had. More than stuck, Heather felt lost and confused. She felt she wasn't good enough and wasn't "doing it right," struggling to find clients and start a coaching business.

Heather was being hard on herself, comparing herself to others and judging herself to be inadequate. She felt alone and hopeless.

In a coaching session with Heather we began to explore what she truly wanted for her life: the values she lived by, the standards she wanted to live up to and the work she really wanted to do. Not surprisingly, we discovered that she didn't want to build her own coaching practice and be an entrepreneur.

The work Heather truly wanted was to work as a coach within a company to help people and teams be their best. Developing talent and improving productivity is a key function in every company. Heather didn't want to run a business. She wanted security and to see the difference she was making in people's lives every day.

Heather's dream for coaching highlights the many ways to use our skills to help people make conscious choices. She just wanted to help people and do the work she loves. Being able to admit that to herself and accept it was huge.

There is always a real reason why you feel stuck, lost or confused. When you uncover the source of the block, why something desired is not happening or why something undesired keeps occurring, you're able to change direction and align yourself with your true path to your authentic life.

***

A perfect example of unconscious reactions to change is how relationships evolve after the birth of a baby. I held a workshop for moms at a mother's center where we focused on communication after baby's arrival.

The moms were in total agreement when asked to describe their lives with baby: they felt alone at home, cut off from colleagues and friends, often struggling to adapt to the baby. They felt their lives had changed drastically whereas their partners' lives were virtually unchanged.

Many mothers felt that their husbands didn't care as much as they did, downplaying their contribution and struggles. One woman told us that the first chance her husband had for time off, he wanted to go hunting for five days instead of staying home to help her. She felt he was shirking his responsibility, leaving her solely responsible for the baby.

I asked the women to list their values – what was important to them and how things had changed. I wanted them to be clear about who they had become as moms and how each of them wanted to live their lives now.

Next I asked them if they thought their partners knew their values and what was important to them since their babies were born. Each of them acknowledged that they hadn't had that conversation with their husbands. Lack of communication with their partners was common to all the moms. Their 'aha' moment came when they realized that they just expected their husbands to know how their lives had changed and how they felt.

The women started to realize that they were playing the blame game instead of communicating, accusing their husbands of not being or doing enough, causing their partners to be defensive and distancing themselves.

The moms hadn't thought about it from the dads' perspective, how they might be lost and questioning themselves about their role with mom and baby. Moms have such a close tie with their babies – dads can't breastfeed and stressed out moms often make it hard for men to find their place in the new family dynamic.

I shifted the moms' perspectives by asking probing questions about their own behavior at home and with their spouse: how they respond to situations, whether they leave space for their spouse to help, how they react when baby cries, etc. The women went home that day with a valuable shift in their thinking. By making a conscious choice to examine their values and discuss them with their partners, they were able to take back their power and build a stronger relationship with themselves, their husbands and their babies.

***

Health is a key reason why people seek out the help of a life coach. Janet was a member of my iPEC Canada Accredited Coaching Program. One day I held a personal coaching meeting with her after an intense session in class. Janet was in her 50s, had struggled with her weight for years, couldn't sustain healthy intimate relationships and she viewed herself as unworthy.

Janet was over-focused on her weight. She couldn't accept herself as she was and hated her body. No matter what she tried, she just couldn't lose weight. Janet was desperate to change. Working together to uncover her values and desires for her life, Janet remembered a story that still gives me shivers today.

As a six-year-old child, Janet became very sick and was losing weight rapidly, to the point where she was hospitalized. Her doctors could not find the cause of her weight loss. One day, as the team of specialists discussed her case at her bedside, Janet could not help but overhear them saying, "We don't know what to do with her. If she continues to lose weight like this, she's going to die."

In that instant, it all became clear. Janet cried as the memory came flooding back to her. She had heard what the doctors said and got scared – she didn't want to die. That precise sentence was imprinted in her subconscious mind and guided her from then on. The life-saving solution of gaining weight so she wouldn't die served Janet well when she was six and ill, but it was not what she needed as an adult.

The subconscious mind is where all of our beliefs passed on by parents, teachers and life experiences are stored. We hold these beliefs as truth and they shape our world. As described by Bruce Lipton in his book *Biology of Belief* (p. 134-135), the subconscious is like a computer's hard drive. We can program anything and the computer will function according to the given instructions. The only way for the computer to do anything different is for us to program something different. Our subconscious mind works in the same way: we need to deprogram what is not working and program it with information that serves us.

Once Janet realized that she could not lose weight because her subconscious was protecting her, she was able to reprogram her belief and take charge of her health.

We changed her focus away from losing weight to being healthy and Janet began to accept her weight. She started to eat healthy food and exercise on a regular basis (respecting her body's capacity and limits). As she started to take good care of herself, she felt better about who she was and started to lose weight.

Change is possible when we confront the belief system that has been leading us in life and ask ourselves if it is true and right for us. Only then can we set out a new belief system that is in alignment with who we really are.

***

Money problems are often a sign of being stuck and out of alignment in your life. One of my regular coaching clients, Jason, was a business owner who was having a tough time financially.

Jason came to me because on the outside his business seemed to be sound, but on the inside it was crumbling. He lacked structure, couldn't get the right people to work for him, was losing money (paying more than necessary, invoices were not sent out, etc.), contracts coming in were not what he wanted, and more.

His business needed serious restructuring but Jason was exhausted. He was working long hours and he couldn't focus. Jason had lost his passion for his business and he needed my help.

I had been coaching him for a while and knew he believed in the law of attraction, so I asked him, "What do you really want here?" Jason's answer changed everything. He replied, "All I want is just enough to get by."

That is exactly what Jason was manifesting, just enough to get by. You see, you can say "I want to be rich," but if the program playing in your subconscious mind is "I just want to get by," this is what you'll create for yourself. The program runs the show!

From there we concentrated on Jason's inner work. What did he really want? What values, beliefs and vision did he have for his business? What needed to go and what needed his focus?

Underneath it all we discovered that as a kid, he had seen his father succeed then fail in business and never recover. His fear of success and subsequent failure was at the root of his unsatisfactory business results. Jason questioned: "Can I be better than my Dad? Is it okay to be better? If I succeed, will I fail too?"

Jason realized that although the core of his business was organizing medical events, his passion was everything to do with event logistics (security, telecommunication needs, venue, etc.). He didn't enjoy the medical part at all. Jason then hired people to manage the medical content and developed the part of his business he was passionate about, giving new life to his company.

Your programming touches every part of your life, from your daily routine to how you behave in all situations: at work, at home, in your marriage, with your kids, friends, family and more. It is your map for interacting with your world.

These people and their stories are all very different, yet they share the same challenge – the programs running their subconscious minds were out of sync with their true selves.

Thoughts are energy; they vibrate at different energy levels. If your thoughts are destructive, they will have a lower vibration. When you have thoughts that are aligned with your core beliefs and values, where you can see possibilities and seize opportunities that feel right for you, they have a higher vibration.

Now just imagine being at a lower energy level. You keep seeing situations where life is bringing you more of what you don't want. If you are avoiding situations and people, procrastinating, feeling frustrated, angry and stressed, your thoughts have a lower energy level and are attracting at that level.

When you change your core beliefs to be in sync with who you truly are, you'll vibrate at a higher energy level. Your actions will reflect your new thoughts and beliefs, sending your high energy out into the world and attracting likeminded energy in people and situations.

That is how we manifest and why it's so important to uncover the real you, whether you're a writer, photographer, life coach or whatever it is you dream of.

Be resourceful and don't be afraid to ask for help. You don't have to do it alone. A certified life and business coach will help you get to the root of the matter.

Follow your natural talents and passions. It starts with the power of choosing: become aware of your beliefs and choose consciously what you want those beliefs to be and who you truly want to be in life. Only then can you start manifesting exactly what you want. That's your personal change revolution to build a conscious life that's just right for only you.

***

Learn more about how Julie Anne can help you build a conscious life by visiting her website:

www.consciouschanges.com/thechange

Or contact Julie Anne at: jac@consciouschanges.com

Kurt A. David

Kurt A. David has lived a life many might envy... former professional athlete, best-selling author, TV personality, keynote speaker, internationally certified sports counselor, and transition consultant to professional & Olympic athletes.

He is the creator of the highly-acclaimed book and TV show, *"From Glory Days"* which chronicles the lives of Hall of Fame, All-Star, and World Champion former professional athletes.

Kurt has vast experience with TV, radio, and print media, and currently resides in Metro Detroit with his wife and two young daughters. Despite his extremely busy schedule, he believes it is important to give back and does so by volunteering his time and resources to the following organizations: Board Trustee to Beyond Sport Integrated – Monze, Zambia (Africa); Advisory Board Member to International Sports Professionals Association – Headquartered in Chicago, Illinois; Supervisory Committee Member to LOC Federal Credit Union – Metro Detroit; Co-creator of the MIND OVER MATTER Bike Event benefitting the Alzheimer's Association; and numerous other local youth assistance and charity events.

As a keynote and workshop speaker, Kurt's presentations are entertaining, educational, and inspiring, and focused on Positive Leadership, Team Work, and Facing Change like a Champion.

My CHANGE

By Kurt David

Imagine this... I'm walking through an airport and getting ready to board a plane for the biggest trip of my life. I mean, this is something I've dreamed for all my life. Suddenly, as I'm settling into my seat I'm overwhelmed with feelings of excitement and feelings of nervousness all at the same time. I'm excited because I am boarding the plane to fly to Europe to play professional basketball (imagine getting paid for something that you absolutely love). I was nervous because I was going to be 5,000 miles away from my family and friends, in a country whose language I didn't speak, and I really didn't know what to expect as far as the basketball.

Move forward in time from those dichotomous feelings, and I'm lying on a cold hardwood floor. As I lay on that floor, I remember the sound of the people in the arena going from a loud roar to a sudden hush, and I vividly recall people whispering all around me. At that moment I realized my life would change... my life would drastically change.

An Old English Idiom states, "Variety is the spice of life." Another tells us, "Change is the only thing constant in life." But what happens when the variety or change occurs in the form of adversity or a major transition in our lives? What happens when our lives advance in a different direction, a new phase so to speak, whether desired or not? Stress, insecurity, uncertainty, and aimlessness can accompany feelings of exhilaration and excitement that one might face while experiencing a change or transition.

You don't need to be a social scientist to know that many changes occur throughout the course of our life. Jobs, relationships, residency, family, incomes, death, loss, and the lists go on. Some changes we seek, and others we avoid like the plague. Regardless, "CHANGE HAPPENS," and the purpose of this chapter is to help embrace the change and adversity we'll often face throughout our life.

I've lived a life many might envy... former professional athlete, highly-regarded author, TV personality, keynote speaker, graduate studies professor, masters level counselor, and transition consultant to world class athletes; but amongst my many, rich experiences have come numerous changes and transitions.

R.U.L.E.S. for Successful Change

Following my athletic glory days, I've since worked with highly-successful individuals, organizations, and businesses that at times face challenges with handling change and transition. For many years I've researched this topic of change, especially as it applies to individuals and businesses. In combination with this research, the work from my TV show with former professional athletes, my counseling work with transitioning professional and Olympic athletes, and my highly-regarded first book, I've discovered that there are five commonalities of success for handling change.

In other words, by implementing these five commonalities or principles when facing change, we can experience success with the change that so often happens in our life.

As a simple mind, I've created a simple acronym for these five principles... R.U.L.E.S.

R.U.L.E.S. and each letter stands for something… each letter means something.

Refocus

The R in the R.U.L.E.S. for successful change stands for Refocus.

Following any change or transition in our lives, it's imperative to refocus. And the best way to refocus is to evaluate our current goals while developing new goals. By doing so, we also develop a new sense of purpose.

As a five-time NHL All-Star and former New York Ranger & Detroit Red Wing, John Ogrodnick began his refocusing long before his professional hockey career ended. While still thriving as a professional athlete, injuries motivated him to begin exploring options for the next phase of his life; and his focus turned razor sharp when realizing his interest in financial matters. While dabbling with stocks during his playing days in New York, Ogrodnick began to refocus and develop a new set of goals, which included acquiring of a Series 7 license. This refocusing helped John Ogrodnick plan and successfully move into the next phase of his life as a financial advisor.

What happens if you don't plan or refocus your life prior to any change and you're thrust into circumstances that are undesired or unplanned? Perhaps you may not have the luxury of time or planning for this change and a tail-spin could entail, as a result.

Such was the case of the 1,273 breweries in America when the 18th Amendment occurred on January 16, 1920, and they could no longer legally sell their product as a result of Prohibition. As a result, over 80% of the breweries in America went out of business because of their inability to change swiftly enough to survive this drastic and unwanted change. However, one of the surviving 244 companies decided they would not allow this change to close their doors, and refocused their product line from brewing beer to producing corn syrup, root beer, ginger ale, and malt extracts. This company's refocus went so far as making refrigerator, truck, and auto body parts; and as a result of this refocus during adversity, Anheuser-Busch not only endured this drastic change but eventually became the number one brewery in the world, employing over 30,000 employees and having over $20 billion in annual sales.

Whether the change is desired, planned, or adverse, a refocus is the first step in success. And the best way to refocus is to evaluate your current goals while establishing new goals; and by doing so a new passion and purpose may also be created.

Using Network

The U in the R.U.L.E.S. for successful change stands for Using Network.

Professional athletes naturally develop a vast network of people by the end of their playing careers, regardless of whether these relationships are sought or not, a byproduct of their career is a large network of people.

Early on, I discovered that using my network is a beneficial asset during transition from sports, especially, when strategically aligning with people aligned with my goals.

Before I proceed, please allow me to make clear that I am not advocating the use and abuse of people, but actually the development of win-win relationships, especially when those relationships are aligned with common goals.

As an example, former UCLA standout and professional football player Mel Farr, developed a vast network of people throughout his playing career. One of the people in his network happened to be a gentleman by the name of William Clay Ford who just happened to own the Ford Motor Company AND the pro football team for which he played. Mel Farr knew that football would not last forever, and prior to the end of his professional career, his refocus included the desire to someday own an auto dealership. Needless to say, Mel's relationship with William Clay Ford made for an extremely integral use of his network and ultimate ownership of not simply one dealership, but enough dealerships to make Mel Farr the #1 African-American businessmen in America, worth over $600 million, at the peak of his business career.

Not everyone's network may allow for such a mutually beneficial relationship as Mel Farr and William Clay Ford, but it became clear to Anheuser-Busch that tapping into an already existing network of distribution during their battle to survive 13 years of Prohibition, allowed their refocused product line to continue their success.

Whether a professional athlete or brewery, by strategically Using our Network of relationships we can have success during change.

Let Go

The L in the R.U.L.E.S. for successful change stands for Let Go.

Bar none, the most difficult aspect of transition for world class athletes is letting go. Tenacity and never giving up is in the marrow of every high-caliber athletes' bones, but the ability to let go is challenging for many, and imperative in successfully handling change regardless of the type of transition.

The ability to let go is as individual as the person who seeks it. Case in point is two former world class athletes that handled this aspect of change very differently. One was an Olympic medalist and the other a Major League Baseball pitcher. Both former clients of mine and facing the end of their careers quite differently. For the Olympic medalist it took six months to decide if he would be done and let go of his glory days. In contrast, less than one week following the professional baseball pitcher's release during spring training he was fully refocused, tapping into his network, and completely letting go of his identity as a professional athlete.

As a large organizational, Ford Motor Company held onto a marketing campaign and slogan for many years stating, "Quality is Job #1." However, during a severe downturn in sales, the company was faced with the reality that they were not really practicing what they preached. As told directly to me by a Ford executive, "We had to come to grips with the fact that we were not living up to this slogan, and let it go." Because Ford Motor Company was able to let go of the fact that quality really wasn't job #1, they were able to begin producing quality vehicles that would compete in a world market, seeing over 25% growth and over $40 billion profit in the past five years.

Whether a professional athlete or world-wide corporation, letting go of past failures AND successes allows us to move forward when facing change.

Execute

The E in the R.U.L.E.S. for successful change stands for Execute.

One of the winningest college coaches of all time once told me, "Knowing what to do isn't good enough if we don't have the discipline to do it." In other words, we need to execute, and when it comes to successfully managing change, we need to execute over and over again.

Upon returning to Rome from war, conquering generals were honored with parades through the streets of the city. During the acco-

My Change

lades, it is told that someone would be riding in the conquering general's chariot during the parade chirping in their ear, "All glory is fleeting, all glory is fleeting..." thus reminding them of a need to continue their success.

A modern day example of this principle grew up on the rough side of our nation's capital and discovered a sport for which he excelled. Despite his challenging environment, he worked hard and was recognized as a high school All-America in basketball. After high school, he earned a full-ride athletic scholarship to Syracuse University, where he also earned All-America status. He then became a NBA #2 draft pick and his professional career earned him an induction into the NBA Hall of Fame.

After departing professional basketball, he faced much criticism and adversarial comments including, "You're just a dumb jock," and "What are you doing trying to build a business." Despite this adversity, he built a business that produced $500 million annually in revenue following his pro sports career.

Anywhere along the line, this former athlete could have stopped and easily rested on his accomplishments. But he continued his success and eventually became the mayor of a large metropolitan area hit hard by a recessive economy.

From high school All-America, to collegiate All-America, to #2 NBA draft, to NBA Hall of Fame, to $500 million business, to mayor of a metropolitan city... Dave Bing truly understood that 'all glory is fleeting' and continued to execute over and over toward his success during his changes.

Someone

The S in the R.U.L.E.S. for successful change stands for Someone.

As mentioned in the principle of using your network, aligning with people who may assist with the accomplishing of your refocus is important, and finding someone to singularly serve as a mentor is even more imperative.

Greg Kelser was an Academic & Athletic All-American and won a NCAA National Championship with teammate Earvin 'Magic' Johnson. While playing in the NBA, Kelser enjoyed his time being on television and began hanging out in a local studio with a broadcaster he had grown to respect, learning as much as he could about the television industry.

The many years of mentoring by this someone paid off for Greg Kelser during his transition from sports, as he's now accomplished over 25 years of TV broadcasting.

The Ford Motor Company found someone when facing serious financial challenges following the 2008 economic downturn. They turned to an individual who had successfully navigated similar struggles in the auto industry; and this recent mentoring by former Chrysler CEO Lee Iacocca was just another reason that Ford Motor Company was able to experience a recent turnaround and success.

Finding someone to be a mentor is important for successfully facing change.

THE FINAL CHANGE

At some point we will all face a final change: the transition from life to death. Regardless of your faith, creed, religion, or spiritual belief, death is an event that we'll all eventually experience... this is an undeniable fact. We live in a world in which the strong have survived throughout history, but ultimately still pass away.

As someone who works with change and transition, I'd be remiss to overlook this most important final change and how to successfully handle it. I believe this journey first starts with an understanding of what death is, and I'm unable to think of a better definition than what's found in the Merriam-Webster dictionary which states, "Death – a permanent cessation of all vital functions."

I'm certain this definition could be dissected and analyzed to mean much more, but confident we'd all agree on one aspect of this description… it's permanent. Once dead, our body as we know it is not coming back.

Arguably the most famous writer of all time, William Shakespeare, stated on his death bed, "I commend my soul into the hands of God my Creator, hoping and assuredly believing, through the merits of Jesus Christ my Savior, to be a partaker of life everlasting…" Prior to his final change, Shakespeare took heart in the best-selling book of all time and its simple truth that belief in Jesus Christ as Lord and Savior provides eternal life after death. Like William Shakespeare, I'm unable to think of a more successful way to face this final transition.

So regardless of whether you're facing changes as a world class athlete, within an organization, within the family, with your job, or the final transition from this life… by applying these principles you can have success as you face life's changes.

By following my own R.U.L.E.S. for successful change, I've discovered my purpose in life is to help other people. Serving others is what motivates me and creates passion in my life.

To Contact Kurt:

Please allow me an opportunity to serve you by contacting me at: prospeaker@kurtdavid.com

You can find out more about me, my books, my TV show, and my keynote speaking services at: www.kurtdavid.com

I look forward to hearing from you!

Kurt A. David

Marilynn Hughes

Marilynn Hughes founded 'The Out-of-Body Travel Foundation' in 2003, (Mission – Reduce Spiritual and Physical Hunger Worldwide). Marilynn has written 75+ books, 40 magazines and around 15 CD's on Out-of-Body Travel and Comparative Religious Mysticism. These books, along with accompanying music and art, are all available for free download. Marilynn has experienced, researched, written and taught about Out-of-Body Travel and Mysticism since 1987 and has appeared on innumerable radio and television programs to discuss her thousands of out-of-body experiences. She is featured in the documentary film 'The Road to Armageddon,' which was released in the Fall of 2012, and has been included in 'The Encyclopedia of the Unseen World,' (By Constance Heidari, Red Wheel Weiser) in 2009, and 'Extra-Planetary Experiences: Alien Human Contact and the Expansion of Consciousness,' by Dr. Thomas Streicher in 2012.

Marilynn was invited to speak at the 2014 Conference for Consciousness and Human Evolution nine Global Scientists, Humanitarians and Mystics are invited to London to speak about the evolution of human consciousness; Marilynn has been the object of a Scientific Study on Out-of-Body Experiences and a subject in a Scientific Study on XPE, Extra-Planetary Experiences.

Dr. Rudy Schild

Dr. Rudy Schild is an Emeritus research astronomer at the Harvard/Smithsonian Center for Astrophysics, following an extensive career studying Dark Matter, Black Holes, and the fluid mechanical origins of Cosmic Structure. Because of his long association with Dr. John Mack, he has become interested in the formulation of a coherent understanding of a space-time in the universe, and is a champion of Dr. Edgar Mitchell's (Apollo 14 Astronautic, Founder of the Institute of Noetic Sciences) quantum hologram formulation of the nature of existence and reality. As Editor-in-Chief of the Journal of Cosmology, he has attempted to broaden the scope of scientific inquiry to include the nature of consciousness and the Universe of Universes. His astronomy website is https://www.cfa.harvard.edu/~rschild/.

The Science for Moral Law

By Marilynn Hughes and Dr. Rudy Schild

This inquiry between Dr. Rudy Schild and myself began after a discussion we'd been having on new discoveries in science (on his end) and mysticism (on my own). Dr. Schild had mentioned in one of these conversations that there was science to support a moral law, which holds the fabric of the universe in place and is consistently significant within its workings and operations. My interest was piqued. I asked him to explain the science supporting moral law and this was his reply.

"As science ponders the apparent conclusion that the Universe seems to have been constructed with fine tuning for a uniform cloud of expanding gas, the Big Bang, to become galaxies, stars, planets and physical sentient beings, it is increasingly difficult for science to avoid noticing that the universe seems to have been fine-tuned for this purpose. As scientists, we notice that the Universe is fundamentally defined by a dozen arbitrary numbers, which seem to have no relationship to each other, but which seem to have worked out perfectly. And if the numbers were to differ from the values observed, the amazing result of sentient life could not have occurred. The numbers I refer to are the speed of light, c, the Planck constant, h, the Newton gravitational constant, g, the mean ratio of protons to neutrons in our atoms, phi, the electron charge, e, etc. We find that if any of these numbers were off of their observed values by a tiny amount, like increased by 1%, then the complex sequence of events couldn't have worked. For example, if the gravitational constant g were a tiny bit larger, then black holes would not have originated soon enough for their amazing consciousness-supporting presence to carry our memory and embody our souls.

So we can easily find ourselves slipping into the conclusion that the purpose of the Universe is for physical structure to occur, so that sentient life can thrive. Some would say, getting farther away from precepts of physical science alone, that the purpose is for love to originate and encompass the creation, for the celebration of the Creator.

If so, then we have a foundational basis for the moral law that must guide us. Everything that we do must foster and support the development of life, and the protection of the natural environment given to it by its Creator. We easily conclude that the ideal human life encourages all living beings, great and small, and recognize their places and needs. And how can we not appreciate and thank our Creator, and do we not glorify Him and his creation, by deeper inspection and study of it all?" Dr. Rudy Schild

So let me share my thought process with you when I first read Dr. Schild's response.

If this is true... what does that tell us? What does this *really* mean for all of us?

We know we are mortal beings. We know we will die. We know our existence *here* is temporary. Yet most of us would concur that the soul is immortal and lives eternally.

So if this is true, and **all creation** has been designed for the sole purpose of physical embodiment . . . why? Why would something so important also be so temporary?

Further, if this is true, it throws everything materialists have believed about physical reality on its heels. But yet, **at the same time**, it throws much of what religion, mysticism and the spiritual beliefs of many peoples on its heels, as well. In essence, Dr. Schild has just rocked all of our worlds!

By demonstrating that the physical journey is more important - so relevant as to require the entire universal system to be based on perfect mathematical accuracy to ensure this outcome – whichever camp you come from, material or spiritual, your world has been completely changed by this scientific revelation.

In Dr. Schild's discoveries, we find an argument for a congruency to life; laws which could define forward, backward and steady action, and thus, motion, which could translate into mathematical formulas which can show expansion, retraction or consistent motion within the movement of universal creation.

Imagine this. Imagine how important this possibility has suddenly become in your world and mine. If actions have mathematical, and thus, energetic import, what does this mean about you and me?

More than anything, it would show us that everything that we do has meaning, purpose, substance and truth. It would demonstrate that the choices and decisions we make have universal implications which could affect our own world and worlds beyond our own that we cannot yet even imagine. It gives a substantive reality to everything we think, say, do or choose not to do.

Now, many of us have heard of ideas thrown around like the laws of abundance and the laws of attraction. But what if there is something inherently flawed in these concepts simply because of a misunderstanding on our part of what either of these actualities represent?

The laws of abundance as often stated, are very often focused on financial outcomes. But what is true abundance really? Is it money, or is it a loving family? Is abundance having everything you want in this world we know is temporary, or having something more . . . perhaps something that would transcend this temporary world when it was your time to cross over into the other?

The laws of attraction are often again stated as bringing towards us what we believe that we want in this temporary world. But yet, do we really know what we want or what would give us a sense of satisfaction, well-being or goodwill? Do we know whether that which we are attracted to will bring us pain or a sense of peace? Again, would you wish to draw to yourself those things which are only of this world, or those which could transcend this temporary world when it was your time to cross over into the other?

So, how do you know if the abundance you seek will actually fulfill your life, or the attractions that you currently pursue will be of any eternal consequence? These laws seem to contain within them a double-edged sword; that which could be deemed positive mixed with that which could be deemed negative in your life... and that very element annuls their worth.

Allow me to introduce you to an old law, one which mystics have inquired of for thousands of years, but much of humanity has failed to pursue in a truly tangible way and in a consistent manner. But the pursuit of this law contains within it everything... the law of contentment.

Going back to Dr. Schild's comments, in particular "the purpose is for love to originate and encompass the creation, for the celebration of the Creator."

How familiar is this to those of us who have kept up with studies on near death experiences? How familiar is this to those of us who have studied the ancient sacred texts of mystics throughout the ages? How familiar to those who have experienced out-of-body travel or other forms of mystical interchange with things divine?

Although there is more than one common denominator in all of these experiences, for the sake of our subject, let us focus on just the one – love.

Near death experiencers, mystics and others who have experienced other-worldly phenomena, universally proclaim the unconditional love of the great Divine, the Universe, God – whatever they may choose to call it. They are encompassed within it. And it is considered one of the criteria of a valid near death experience to look upon the life of the individual who has experienced it and observe whether or not their life has drastically changed.

And this is so because so many near death experiencers come back with an enhanced awareness of those things within the context of their lives which promoted the universal good, and those things which did not. In my own near death experience, the Lord Jesus Christ revealed to me that the purpose of our earthly existence here was simple. It was to go from a state of selfishness towards selflessness...

How many of us have heard the bible saying which states very simply that we should do good and avoid evil?

> *"Seek good and not evil, that ye may live. Hate the evil and love the good."* Amos 5:14-15

Why? Is it because there is a choice between expansion and contraction involved within those choices? Perhaps we are to avoid evil because it causes a contraction.

And what about this?

> *"Woe unto them that call evil good and good evil; that put darkness for light."* Isaiah 5:20

Why 'Woe?' Could it be that if we call good evil or evil good, we are promoting to those who hear us a contraction, while giving off the impression that we encouraging an expansion? And 'Woe' to us who mislead others into doing the opposite of that which they may sincerely intend?

Perhaps these warnings in biblical and other ancient texts are there because there is a universal and eternal law at stake which affects the expansion and contraction of the universe? Perhaps, in being warned to do good and to take the time to form our consciences in a manner which supports our ability to discern that which is good from that which is evil, we are being directed to move within the universal law of love which naturally (again through eternal law) leads to contentment?

How does this lead to contentment?

Well, we have already ascertained that we live a temporal world which lasts but a short time. We will all die; our existence here is temporary. We have already ascertained from Dr. Schild's comments that it is quite possible that the entire universe was created with the purpose of physical creation at its summit. These almost seem to contradict one another, yet they do not.

Let us digress. What is the secret of the saints?

How much do we really control in our lives here in this temporary existence? And what does come with us when we leave this realm and return to the other side?

We control only how much we love… and we retain only the love we engender ***and*** our deeds, be they good, evil, indifferent… be they expansive, contractive or simply sustaining.

The secret of the saints is that they chose to do good and avoid evil. And as long as they were doing this; there was nothing that could be done to them which could affect their contentment. In the fires of persecution, although it would be irresponsible to say they didn't experience pain, fear, hardship or hurt, we can say they experienced peace. Because they were at peace with God.

But who is God if not the center and creator of this universe? And isn't this universe demonstrating to us, in all of these mathematical constants which Dr. Schild so skillfully merged and explained for us, a Presence which requires our understanding? And do not these constants show a unity and plan which require absolute precision? And the saints demonstrated that precision in their actions by recognizing that their only power within this physical universe - the physical constraint of our mortal lives - was their conscious and continual choice to do good and avoid evil.

Do good, avoid evil, contentment arises. This is a thought which is contained within, yet transcends and unites all world religious and spiritual thought.

Despite all the relativism our world has provided to us, can we not all agree that in our heart of hearts we all know the difference between that which is good and that which is evil? We know the difference between actions which cause expansion and those which cause retraction, do we not? And I would venture to say that we know that which provides sustenance and those things which might be called 'lukewarm' which cause diminution due to a lack of any action, would you agree?

And the great thing about such things, as well, is that our universe has provided many mystical and ascetical theologians who can help us to define such matters and continue to form our conscience in a manner which would support the universal law of love, rather than contradict it in the name of our own desires or pleasures.

Perhaps what we should also look more closely upon, those desires and pleasures of which we remain so attached, because in the light of the unconditional love of an Almighty God and a universal sphere of intelligence which presses us to higher modes of operation and stimulus, is it conceivable that these very things we believe we want and need are concealing from us the true and great dignity of humanity as created by an intelligence infinitely above and beyond them?

One cannot help but wonder if the simple name God gives to Himself in the Old Testament, 'I Am,' conceals a secret regarding the eternal law of contentment. Perhaps it is our need to define ourselves and others, to define world and personal events within a context; and maybe even our need to contain within the fragments of an unimaginative intelligence a confined designation which may have absolutely no meaning and bear no truth in the eternal sense, which keeps the soul in an eternal state of desiring and deprives it of peace.

A contented life results from an illumination of the soul that incorporates resonance with good, and hence with the purpose of the diadem of the universe. Good and evil vibrate with an ***actual physical*** quantum presence in our objective universe and in the soul. Bringing the two together in an act of consciousness generates creates a luminescence and compatible resonance with the actual ***purpose*** of the Universe. Because of this resonation within the context of the higher, finer vibrational spheres of will, motion and stringent access to that which is, the individual soul immediately experiences the arising of contentment. Other souls, other people, can touch into this resonation generated by an individual, and sometimes without even knowing why, find themselves swept up in a sudden onset of contentment, peace or well-being. This palpable resonance and alignment to the Eternal Soul of good and universal intention, design or schema is what brings us into the ecstatic experience.

The Change 3

For those of us who have been borne into mysticism throughout the ages, there is a desiring that emanates from desirelessness, a striving which is immersed in not striving, and a contentment which derives from simply moving within the universal initiation of expansion. By thus uniting with and merging the forces of a single soul with that of a greater and boundless reality, the soul melts into an endless sea of cosmic delights and goodnesses. All things become one... contentment arises.

At almost all funerals, you will hear read the 23rd Psalm of David. Why is this? Do you know? It is the secret that everybody is seeking, yet concealed within the tempered words of a mystical soul who kept it silent and unrearing in its mysteries to those who might not yet understand them. Perhaps you are ready to understand them. Perhaps you are ready now, too.

"The Lord is my shepherd, I shall not want. He maketh me to lie down in green pastures: he leadeth me beside the still waters. He restoreth my soul: he leadeth me in the paths of righteousness for his name's sake. Yea, though I walk through the valley of the shadow of death, I will fear no evil: for thou art with me; thy rod and thy staff they comfort me. Thou preparest a table before me in the presence of mine enemies: thou anointest my head with oil; my cup runneth over. Surely goodness and mercy shall follow me all the days of my life: and I will dwell in the house of the Lord for ever." Psalm 23

Science and the moral law have always been united, but today, let us gather in their joining and announce to the world the excitement and adventure which lays beyond because of this revelation. Our former worlds have passed away, the worlds of those of us who were among the materialists and the worlds of those of us who were among the spiritually minded. And today we have seen something new, something that has engaged us in a rapid encounter with the universal intelligence which created us for this moment.

And we may now choose that this moment will bear fruit in every single one of our lives because it really is that simple.

Love one another. Do good, avoid evil... allow contentment to arise.

Namaste (I Bow to the Divine in You)

– Hindu Greeting

Jai Jinendra (Victory over Sustainable Happiness)

- Jainist Greeting

Sat Sriakaal (The Eternal Truth)

- Sikh Greeting

Shalom Alechum (Peace Be Upon You)

- Jewish Greeting

Hamazor Hama Ashobed (I am fine and hope you are, too)

– Zoroastrian Greeting

Buddha Namo (In the Name of the Buddha)

– Buddhist Greeting

My Peace I Give You, My Peace I Leave with you

- Words of Christ

Peace be With You

- Christian Greeting

As- Salaam-o-Alaikum (As Peace be Upon You)

The Change 3

– Islamic Greeting

Allah Abho (Glorious God)

– Baha'i Greeting

"The Highest Good, pleased in Itself alone, made man good, and for Good, and gave him this place as an earnest of eternal peace. By his own fault, man did not dwell here long." Dante's Purgatorio, Words of Matelda regarding the Original Earthly Paradise

"My grace is sufficient for thee: for my strength is made perfect in weakness." 2 Corinthians 12:9

To Contact Marilynn Hughes and Dr. Rudy Schild:

The Out-of-Body Travel Foundation, http://outofbodytravel.org

http://outofbodytravel.org/reviewsandbio.html,

http://outofbodytravel.org/appearances.html,

https://www.facebook.com/pages/The-Out-of-Body-Travel-Foundation-Traveling-at-the-Speed-of-Light/136172106452268,

https://www.linkedin.com/profile/view?id=28563110&trk=nav_responsive_tab_profile

Mark Skovron

Mark Skovron has achieved extraordinary levels of success many times over.

As a successful businessman, coach, author, and philanthropist, Mark originally excelled as a successful executive for several of the best-known brands in Corporate America before discovering his passion for being a Free Agent and helping others achieve the same.

For over 25 years, Mark has been the founder of several businesses in multiple industries, and personally distinguished himself as a Top 1% earner worldwide.

Mark's current business has become a Top 25 Company in just four years and already produced many $100k earners.

Mark authored the best-selling CD and online course, "Take Charge of Your Life."

For his results, Mark has been featured in many publications including Your Business At Home, Network Marketing Lifestyles and Millionaire Magazine, as well as the Co-Author of several books and articles.

A master at teaching others how to build profitable independent enterprises, Mark's absolute gift is in showing others how to build businesses from their home, replace career incomes, live out their passions and live life on their terms. As he likes to declare, "It is time for the Free Agent Revolution."

The Free Agent Revolution

By Mark Skovron

Where Did They All Go?

The EVP for one of the largest real estate companies in the country abruptly resigns after many years. A hair stylist walks out of her salon after 27 years, never to return. A supervisor for one of the largest package delivery companies walks away, and doesn't look back.

A teacher, a corporate sales rep for a leading airline, an executive for one of the county's largest banks, an I.T. systems expert with a major corporation, and millions of others are walking away from top careers at an unprecedented rate.

Some are being forced out, some are simply opting out. Either way, they are choosing new unchartered territory for themselves. And life is becoming the best it has ever been for them and their families.

They are your co-workers, relatives, friends, neighbors, and those you never met.

What are these people doing, where are they going, and what caused their sudden departure from their previous 40-year plan?

They've all joined the ranks of the *Free Agent Revolution*.

Free Agent (definition)

> *A person who is able to act freely without being controlled by someone else.*

Revolution (definition)

> *A sudden, extreme, or complete change in the way people live, work, etc.*

Susan and Gary Walsh live in Columbia, S.C. Susan spent 27 years standing on her feet 80 hours weekly in a salon styling hair, doing her part in providing for her family.

Then one day, a woman shared an idea about a product and a compensation plan within the network marketing industry.

Susan immediately seized upon the new venture, somehow finding extra hours to sell and market the product while she styled hair. With one son in dental school, Susan's first goal was an extra $5,000 a month.

The part time opportunity paid off and much more than Susan originally ever imagined. She recruited others to also sell, and built an international organization. Her direct sales company, The 5 Star Marketing Group, has generated over $9 million in commissions to her in the past two decades, and Susan has coached many others to millionaire status. Susan will never again be anything other than a Free Agent.

The Honeymoon Is Over

Allow me to be perfectly honest and clear up front. This chapter is designed to be disruptive. Once you read this, it is doubtful that you will ever feel or think about your job or career the same way again.

But I owe it to you to tell you the truth. I am sounding the alarm in the town square.

I'll try and speak without offending – and you try and read without defending.

There is a revolution that is going on in America. It was inevitable considering that people have grown weary of 60+ hour work weeks, taking homework to do in the evening and on weekends, having little to no vacation time, and dysfunctional workplaces filled with corporate politics.

Workers are waking up to the fact that there is no longer any security or commitment to be gained in the outdated model of employment.

The movement of millions of Americans away from the old relationship of employment and into a Free Agent mode is the result of many things. Probably one of the main drivers is the great socioeconomic changes that have occurred in the past ten years.

Individuals are reassessing their futures and being forced to redefine the meaning of security, career, rewards and develop new ways of not just surviving but thriving in the new caste system we find ourselves in today.

Zik Stewart was employed in real estate while Jerri, his wife, was a well-respected teacher. Their combined incomes supported their family and they enjoyed what they did. But, there was never much discretionary income for those extra things that everyone wants.

A fellow teacher of Jerri's mentioned that they were marketing life insurance on a part time basis for extra income. Once Jerri told Zik, they both decided to give it a try.

The Change 3

"We started selling insurance on a part time basis while keeping our full time jobs," said Jerri. Zik adds, "We worked that secondary income stream for three years before we were both able to become full time."

Since then, their Free Agent business has changed and they became Home-Based Business Consultants. They have independent contracts with two different companies which have produced multi-millions in earnings over the past 30 years, and they have since semi-retired to a beautiful all-inclusive community in Hilton Head, S.C.

What About Security?

Wake up! Try not producing for a week, a month or 3 months at your "secure" job. Just how long do you imagine they will they keep you on the payroll?

It is time you realize that all you have is a week-to-week renewable contract and you are completely disposable. "Right Sizing," corporations call it. It is downsizing that ultimately leads to capsizing of your family's income, budget, and dreams. That's why it is so important to have a back-up plan.

I personally know of one company that appeared for several years in a row on Fortune's List of the 'Top 100 Companies in America to Work For.' As employers go, they did have a reputation for treating their co-workers better than most.

Then the time came that the original investors were courted by a bigger, more powerful company that wanted to buy this top company and add it to its established distribution system.

Offers were made and accepted pending one thing happening: employee compensation reduction.

The company being purchased had about 800 Sales Representatives, who had great jobs, working Monday through Friday from 9 to 5 for compensation between $70 - $150k. Not a bad gig, right?

Just before the acquisition was complete, and in order to 'shape the selling company's numbers,' Sales Managers were commanded to call their Sales Representatives in and inform them that their position, or rather the title, was being eliminated.

It just so happened though, that the same company was conveniently hiring for a 'new' position – a title that had never existed before: Customer Service Representative. The job description was the same exact description as the now evaporated Sales Representative position.

All previous Sales Reps were encouraged to apply, as they were obviously qualified.

The only difference was the title, and that the compensation for the 'new position,' was now at approximately $30,000 a year, about one half to one third of the previous job.

And you know what? Most of the Sales Reps did apply and were hired to do the same job for much lower income. After all, it was either that, or go stand in the unemployment line. Unethical – perhaps. unfair and uncaring – definitely. But this is legal and now the norm.

Scott Smith was an inside sales manager at one of the country's largest banks and in his twenties when he got his wake up call. Scott worked for the bank for a couple of years before being called into his supervisor's office for 'one of those chats.'

His offense? A ninety year old bank customer who didn't quite understand all the workings of her account, accrued 30 NSF fees for a total of $900. While in the bank, Scott reached out to her children to enlist their assistance in getting their mothers account balanced and keeping it that way.

In the meantime, in the spirit of great customer service, not to mention being a kind human gesture, Scott dispensed with all but three of the NSF fees bringing her total owed down to $90.

But Scott's manager explained the bank's profits should come before any customer, and gave Scott his first written warning. When Scott objected, the manager informed Scott that perhaps he should look to some other source for employment.

With zero entrepreneurial skills, and no money, Scott got a 1099 self-employment contract with a company selling medical devices and became a part of the Free Agent Revolution.

Scott moved from Alabama to Florida and began to work his new territory. He racked up thousands of dollars on his credit cards and lived essentially out of his truck while building his business. After 6 months, Scott was close to the $100,000 a year pace.

Since then, Scott has taken his Free Agent model into overdrive and is now the owner of six businesses and counting. He and his wife Diana, and their children, live in a very spacious home in Tampa, Florida, and life just keeps getting better.

Work for a Purpose and Not Just a Paycheck

I like to say, that happy is the man or woman who both works and plays and yet cannot tell the difference.

Sure, there are some very fortunate people who are 'called' to what they do.

Perhaps they are the clergy, doctors, nurses, teachers or the like. They don't work just for their paycheck. These people really love what they do.

But that is the minority I assure you.

Even if you are compensated well for your career, most people surveyed have said that they would gladly accept and adapt to less pay for more quality time with their family and doing those things that they love.

One of my best friends, Martha Kemper always likes to say, and so I want to suggest to you, "that you can actually have it all."

Dave and Jill Myers live in the small town of Eureka, Missouri. After college, Dave found very highly compensated work with his degree and skills as an I.T. expert running technology departments for 20 years, earning him significant mid-six figures.

"I started to look around for something new that would allow me more freedom and flexibility," says Dave.

The first thing that popped up on Dave's radar was the mobile technology boom. Text to mobile for marketing then led Dave with his skills to web design, and that's when Dave joined the Free Agent Revolution and launched his own business.

Dave now comes and goes as he decides, eats lunch with his wife every day, and is at every sporting and school event that his children are involved with.

In just 3 years, Dave's income started leveling out, and he's back to the earnings he previously enjoyed in Corporate America.

"While I am still working to build a portfolio of business accounts so that my residual income is secure," Dave reflects, "My family is the most important thing in the world to me, so even in lean months, it's worth it."

Ready, Set, Go!

Being a Free Agent myself, having started several successful companies, and in my role as a Free Agent Coach (See: www.FreeAgentRevolution.com), I speak to people every week who want to join the Free Agent Revolution, but just don't know how to get started.

Although there is much more detail on the website, the first questions to ask are:

1. What is it that you truly love?

2. What is it that you definitely have a natural skill set for?

Gregg and Tori Sturz make their home in Kennesaw, Georgia, with their children and have found a way to generate a generous income by doing what they love.

After 20 years as a supervisor for UPS, with a generous income, great benefits, and the image of security, Gregg says, "I always had a desire to be more, achieve more, and make a difference for others."

Despite working for a company that many people would gladly work with forever, Gregg wanted, needed, to be involved in something he loved. But what was that to be?

Through the years, Gregg's Free Agent Revolution has taken many forms and paths.

Gregg has started and sold several businesses in the health and wellness industries, and recently just started a healthy pet care business specializing in natural and safe foods, treats and vitamins for pets.

Gregg says, "Tori's passion is about the pets, while I thrive on exploring and creating different businesses for myself and others."

Anna Marques is a member of the Free Agent Revolution out of Dunedin, Florida. Although she has a life-partner, she began her business with her brother Dino.

Anna's background and talents were in contracted management and as a business broker. She decided one day that she had her fill of the corporate world and immediately formed a business plan around what she was great at and already possessed the skills and experience for.

She and Dino, as well as Anna's life-partner Bill, parlayed those previous skill sets into a similar business model and formed Member Benefits Alliance, Inc. The company is an intermediary and contracts with businesses and buyers providing pre-negotiated discounts and acts as a buying club while directing revenue dollars toward businesses that need them.

Anna is doing much of the 'same type of work,' but this time as a Free Agent.

Before joining the Free Agent Revolution, you should do your research. Use our website for all of the free resources and tools available.

But eventually, and the sooner the better, you just simply have to start.

The stories you have read so far will be tugging at you, if you are destined to join our Free Agent Revolution.

Just remember that in the Free Agent world, the few who do (action) become the envy of the many who only stand by and watch.

Build A Support System

One of the most important things that you can do once you decide that the path of the Free Agent is for you, is to build a support system around you, that becomes stronger than any adversity or challenge will be.

Ricky Barnett form Ogden, Utah formed a plan with his wife Sherry to become a Free Agent.

Ricky served in the Armed Forces, has been a group home manager, a counselor and then a carpenter. These are all honorable professions, but not necessarily the resume that some of our other Free Agents possessed.

But in his heart, Ricky had a white-hot obsession for more freedom, to be able to call his own shots, and be able to build up a consistent residual income for the future.

So while trying out different business models, some of which did not take off by the way, Ricky did discover the most important ingredient was to surround and immerse himself in a support and personal growth system that would keep him focused on his goal.

<u>This point cannot be overstated – and is in my opinion, the most important element in whether or not you will succeed in the Free Agent Revolution, but alas, is often ignored.</u>

Ricky went all the way.

He cut off or limited relationships with people who were committed to discouraging him.

He immersed himself every single day in books and audios to reinforce his vision, and built up a strong state of mind.

"I raised my determination and persistence level above my distraction level," Ricky says.

Ricky adds, "I listened to the greats, Jim Rohn, Jim Britt and Jim Lutes. I read the greats, Brian Tracy, Norman Vincent Peale, Og Mandingo and Stephen Covey. And I enrolled Mark Skovron and Jeff Peltin to coach me and gave them permission to not hold back."

Ricky has carried a small 'gratitude rock' with him for many years. The weight, and feel of it every day reminds him that no matter what, to have an attitude of gratitude.

Never Give Up

You must understand that successful people do what they need to do whether they feel like it or not. There are two types of people in this world: men and women of action, and everyone else.

So your breakout into the wonderfully rewarding world of the Free Agent Revolution cannot just be about good ideas, it's about making good ideas happen!

If you are not willing to do the things that it takes to cause your project to succeed, you might as well not even begin. And it is essential that you understand that things won't always happen on your timetable.

Becoming a Free Agent is a Revolution because you are doing something that is disruptive by nature, and many people will never even attempt.

Ples Bruce and his spouse Kameelah from Atlanta, Georgia, were early adopters and joined the Free Agent Revolution years ago, before it was the movement that it is today.

The Change 3

Ples spent many years working in corporate sales for one of the nation's largest airlines.

Despite earning a great living and having many benefits that most would love to have, Ples says, "I wanted the opportunity to create a residual income in a business model that allowed me to work whenever I wanted to."

So Ples formed Venture Head, his Free Agent business model. Although he still works full time for the airline, he also works full time for his own business. Now those hours are quite the commitment, especially after a couple years, but it is all starting to come together for him now. "By joining the Free Agent Revolution," Ples explains, "I have the opportunity to gain control of my income. And when you control your income, you can finally have true security… and that's called freedom."

There is a great quote, one of my favorites, by Jim Rohn:

"Resolve says, I will. The man says, I will climb this mountain. They told me it is too high, too far, too steep, too rocky and too difficult. But it's my mountain. I will climb it. You will soon see me waving from the top or dead on the side from trying."

It's Never Too Late to Start

I've personally been a part of the Free Agent Revolution for over 25 years.

During that time, I have had the privilege of knowing, partnering with, coaching or witnessing the success of all of the people that you have been reading about. I am the better person for my experiences with each of them. Their Free Agent Revolutions have called out the best in me and constantly reminded me why this movement is so important and life-changing for so many.

The Free Agent Revolution

I've watched individuals in their twenties become Free Agents, and some in their eighties.

Don Martin from Atlanta, Georgia is certainly not in his eighties, but he's not in his twenties either. You see, Don spent an entire career in real estate, much of that time as an EVP for Century 21 International Headquarters.

But when Don retired 7 years ago, he still wasn't ready to stop working. So, he formed his company, the U.S. Business Network, and has been a paid executive business coach helping others to launch both for-profits and nonprofits, very successfully for years.

He is a highly sought-out coach, mentor and business building mastermind; and the number of successful businesses that Don has partnered with to launch can't be counted.

So Don's a guy who has it all, had it all early on, retired, but just won't stop building.

He proves that it's never too late to join the Free Agent Revolution.

The Finish Line

Ken Turbow and his life-partner Robert have homes in Sarasota and Pensacola, Florida.

Ken excelled at his career in manufacturing management, becoming the youngest VP in three separate companies. But corporate takeovers and mergers would take their toll and Ken joined the Free Agent Revolution when he started working part time in direct sales. Ken now owns a distributorship with a direct sales healthy chocolates company. "Once I got a taste of being my own boss, I never once thought about going back to Corporate America," Ken reflects.

The Change 3

It's been 21 years since Ken told his employer that their services were no longer needed. Ken's business has always made him over $100,000 a year, with his highest month at $80,000 in earnings.

Becoming a part of the Free Agent Revolution is not something you do instead of working. It is simply a different way of working, and for different reasons, and for different results.

In most cases, Free Agents begin part time, so the hours spent in the development of your business model are in addition to your regular employment.

Being a Free Agent isn't meant for everyone, in fact, it's not for most people; although it is my opinion that everyone, and I mean everyone ought to have a back-up plan.

But those for whom it is their calling, it is literally a dream come true.

The Free Agent Revolution is a claim you stake, then dig for relentlessly, defend against no matter what, and put your whole self into to be at cause for, it's manifestation.

If you're truly a Free Agent 'type,' you'll know it, because your thirst for it will burn constantly and you'll never be truly happy until you are on that journey.

You should know two things as you consider your own Free Agent Revolution. First, it will be at least 10 times harder than you think, or want it to be, but when you achieve that kind of freedom, and become the true captain of your destiny forever, I promise you that it will be 1,000 times better than you ever imagined.

To Contact Mark:

www.FreeAgentRevolution.com

Mark will consult with you at no charge:

Direct: (727) 667-4300

Mark@MarkSkovron.com

Michael E. Schmidlen

Michael E. Schmidlen is a serial solo entrepreneur who has successfully run his multimillion dollar, home-based business for over 20 years. Michael is currently working on finishing his first book, *THE Underwear Entrepreneur - The Definitive Guide to Working from Home*, where he shares his many business experiences and unique stories. The book is designed to be a blueprint for other small business owners, would-be entrepreneurs and start-ups to beat the overwhelming odds to create a successful, thriving small business model.

Michael was named as one of Colorado Biz Magazine's "Top 25 Most Powerful Sales People" in January, 2011, issue.

He was profiled on "Heartbeat of America," hosted by William Shatner.

He was listed in COBiz Magazine "Top 250 Private Companies" list in 2007, ranked #204; in 2008, ranked #184. He was ranked #232 in 2008, Inc. Magazines: "Inc. 500 list of the fastest-growing private companies in America."

He is also currently the Publisher of two new business-themed digital magazines: CRUSHING IT Magazine and UNDERWEAR ENTREPRENEUR Magazine, in addition to running his business.

THE Underwear Entrepreneur Asks You: "Who do YOU Listen to???"

Michael E. Schmidlen

"We are all, right now, living the life we choose." - Peter McWilliams, author

Trying to distill my 30+ years of experience into 3,000 words was a challenge, so I have decided to try to find the BEST of the BEST of the lessons and experiences that I've had during my ongoing career, and to share only the things that have had the biggest impact on my personal growth and development.

I have had the good fortune to be virtually unemployable for over 20 years (and counting)! By that, I mean I've lived a life that many can only dream of, as they toil away at their menial desk job, or their repetitive factory job, or having to deal with a lengthy daily commute, or co-workers they don't like, or bosses who don't appreciate them. I AM an entrepreneur. And I'm not just any old run-of-the-mill entrepreneur, *I AM THE Underwear Entrepreneur.* At this point, I'm sure you're wondering "what exactly does that mean?"

Do I sell underwear? Or am I an heir or family member of the Hanes or Fruit-of-Loom founders? The simple answer is no, but because I have worked from home for over 20 years (*NO commute, NO dress code, NO surly bosses or NO obnoxious co-workers*), I often get to work in the comforts of my underwear, but more often than not in shorts and a t-shirt. Sometimes I even get all dressed-up in jeans and a shirt with a collar (*when I'm feeling really adventurous*). Is it a perfect life (*is anything truly*)? Hardly, like anything there have been good times, very good times, and bad times and very bad times, but there have been far more of the former than the latter. As you would expect, there have been the same trials and tribulations that we all face in our lives, the difference in mine is I have had choices and opportunities that, had I remained working for a large corporation as I did for 9 years early in my career (in my late teens to my late 20's), I would not have had the opportunity to explore and grow as I have. I will caution you that it's not for everyone; we can't all be our own bosses, and running a business requires a substantial amount of time, energy and dedication. There is NO "Plan B" for most successful entrepreneurs. We have to hunt, claw, hustle and scrape for our livelihood and it's the primary reason that we succeed!

> *Who is your coach or mentor?*
>
> *"For those who believe, no proof is necessary.*
>
> *For those who don't believe, no proof is possible."* - Stuart Chase

One of the most important lessons that I've learned is the importance of having a coach and/or a mentor (or many of BOTH). I'm somewhat embarrassed to admit that I hired my first real coach at the end of 2013, a delay that no doubt caused me to endure a lot of unnecessary brain damage by doing things the hard way.

As we continue on the journey that we are all on, one of the most important questions that we all need to figure out is: "Who do YOU listen to?" In our age of information overload and the ability to instantly research virtually any and every subject under the sun - and receive 10's, hundred's, thousands and even millions of potential sources of information - how do you really know who to listen to? Who to trust to provide you with accurate, timely and relevant information? What filters do you use?

While I'm not suggesting that you don't listen to the gurus of the world, I would caution that you do so carefully, and question what their motivation(s) may be with the advice they are offering to you. Also, it's important for you to decide if they and their message are aligned with your personal values and beliefs. Does their message resonate with you? Or does it cause you to pause and give it a second, or more thought(s)? Is your relationship going to be purely a one-sided, transactional one, or is there potential for a deeper connection? I'm at a point in my life and career where I'm no longer interested in engaging in purely transactional relationships. If it's not going to be mutually beneficial and long-term, I'm usually not interested in establishing it to begin with.

Personal coaching has become a very popular and profitable profession in the last decade. I decided that the timing was right for me at this point in my life and professional career to seek the guidance of a professional coach. I was stuck both personally and professionally and needed the input of someone who I could run my challenges by, and who wasn't too close to me, such as a friend or family member, that could educate and enlighten me with their knowledge and insights. Online courses, or CD's and DVD's, have a place in your ongoing education and are great sources of knowledge, but in my opinion they can't compare to the value of personal one-on-one interaction with a coach.

Being an entrepreneur, especially a home-based solo-entrepreneur like myself, can be a very lonely and isolated existence. I found for me that having a professional coach, who could listen and provide me with counsel was both a liberating and life-altering experience and I highly recommend that you engage with one as soon as is possible for you!

With all that said, ultimately you will learn that you need to listen to yourself... Because the thoughts that you think, the words that you use, what and how you feel, as well as the actions that you take or don't take, *are a much better reflection of your subconscious beliefs than any external input you can ever receive.*

> *"Authenticity is a collection of choices that we have to make every day. It's about the choice to show up and be real. The choice to be honest. The choice to let our true selves be seen."* - Brené Brown

Professional or Poseur?

"Trust, but verify" - US President Ronald Reagan

This is a short guide to provide you with some tips on how to spot the poseurs or the professionals. This advice doesn't just apply to the gurus, it also applies to prospective partners and even your customers. While I would never suggest that you distrust everyone, I would caution you to exercise great discretion in whom you decide to support with your hard-earned money. I've seen many, many people fall victim to admiring (and investing in) these poseurs (myself included), because they often appear to be charismatic, powerful, helpful, and most of all interested in you. But when you peek behind the curtain and get to know them personally, you'll find that they're often embellishing, faking or outright lying about a great number of things, such as their:

<u>1. Age.</u>

Poseur: They represent themselves to be younger or older than they actually are, to provide the illusion that they are more successful than they actually are.

Pro: Real experts do not need to deceive people to gain their support.

2. Knowledge.

Poseur: They desperately want you and others to believe in their alleged expertise, but in reality, they don't have the actual hands-on experience, knowledge, or haven't done the necessary heavy lifting to be considered subject matter experts.

Pro: There is no shame in admitting that you don't know something! Real experts practice continuous learning and education.

3. Financial Success.

Poseur: They try to impress you with all sorts of facts and data about how profitable and successful their business is, but the reality is often far different from the picture they are painting for you.

Pro: Real experts know when and what to share and don't need to impress you with their success.

4. Network.

Poseur: They claim to be great super-connectors, but in reality, everything they do is from and for their own self-interest.

Pro: Real experts don't need to name drop to impress people.

5. Their heart and spirit.

Poseur: They pretend to care deeply about the people they're taking money from, but really, they don't care at all. You are nothing more than a meal ticket to them and your relationship will never be anything more than transactional.

Pro: Real experts exhibit their authenticity in everything they do; they practice intellectual honesty, they possess intellectual curiosity and they can't help but to *teach*.

As the quote I mentioned in the beginning of this section advises, I highly suggest that you trust, but verify. Unless you have a personal relationship with someone, or think that you know them well, do some research on Google, LinkedIn, or any source of your choosing or preference to confirm that they are what and who they represent themselves to be.

Again, listen to your intuition or your gut; more often than not they will lead you in the right direction.

"Successful people are always looking for opportunities to help others. Unsuccessful people are always asking, 'What's in it for me?'" - Brian Tracy, Personal and business training author, speaker, and consultant

When the student is ready...

> *"When the student is ready, the teacher will appear"* - Lao Tzu, Chinese Taoist Philosopher, founder of Taoism

Since first learning of this quote a number of years ago, and personally experiencing the meaning on multiple occasions, it has become one of my personal favorites. Some of the many lessons I have learned have certainly been painful (personally, professionally and financially), but I'm better for these experiences, both the good and the bad. You will get to a certain point in your life where you don't want to learn any more life lessons, but the reality is that we all continue to learn throughout our lives, whether we want to or not. The primary lesson I've learned is that it's imperative to continually learn and upgrade your skills, or risk the very real possibility of becoming obsolete. I've been extremely fortunate that I've had people willing to mentor me since I first started in the business world back in the early 80's, some knowingly, and many more unknowingly. The important thing for you to remember is that these people exist for all of us, and if we're willing to be consciously aware of their existence, we can all learn from them and spare ourselves the inevitable brain damage of unnecessarily doing things the hard way. By availing ourselves to these short-cuts, we can significantly shorten the amount of time and energy it takes to become successful.

It is no longer good enough to work on just your professional skills, although that is certainly an important necessity in today's uber-competitive business/market climate; but these skills alone will not help you to achieve all that you're capable of achieving.

One of the common themes that I truly hope that you are picking up on in this chapter is that it's okay to admit you don't have all the answers and to be open to seeking the counsel and guidance of outside experts, whose knowledge and expertise can become paramount to your ultimate success. I have an insatiable appetite to learn, and this is a practice I will continue as long as I'm alive - it's that important.

One of the most important self-development lessons that I've learned is the "Four Stages of Learning" (also known as "The Four Stages of Competence"), a theory posited by psychologist Abraham Maslow in the 1940's.

Here is an overview of "The Four Stages:"

> 1. Unconscious Incompetence: (*You DON'T know that you don't know*)

Knowledge exists that you do not know about, and you have NO clue that this knowledge exists, you are blissfully unaware. Most of us fall under this category many times in our lives, but the good news is that as soon as you become aware of the knowledge that you don't know, you move up to stage 2!

> 2. Conscious Incompetence: (*You know that you DON'T know*)

You are consciously aware that you don't understand or know how to do something, but you do recognize that the deficit exists.

> 3. Conscious Competence: (*You know that you know*)

You understand or know the how, but demonstrating this skill or knowledge requires your concentration. You must practice this new skill or knowledge in order to utilize it, it is not yet second nature.

> 4. Unconscious Competence: (*You know and it happens automatically, often without having to think about it*)

You have had so much practice that the skill or knowledge becomes second nature to you and can be performed effortlessly and easily, often while doing something else (i.e. multi-tasking). You may be able to teach this knowledge or skill(s) to others.

Suffice it to say that you all should aspire to master the skills and knowledge to become *"Unconsciously Competent"* in as many areas as you can!

> *"The secret of getting ahead is getting started. The secret of getting started is breaking your complex overwhelming tasks into small manageable tasks, and then starting on the first one."* - Mark Twain

"Self-Help" or "Shelf-Help?"

> *"Empty the coins in your purse into your mind and your mind will fill your purse with coins."* - Benjamin Franklin

I was recently on a call with my personal business coach, and during our conversation, we were discussing my past efforts and rather impressive collection of self-improvement and self-development books, DVD's and programs, when he used a term that I'd never heard before - "Shelf-Help" - to describe our propensity to buy self-improvement or self-development books and/or products (that we do so with the best of intentions) but that we never use; instead allowing them to collect dust on the shelf. I'm certainly guilty of this behavior, as my friends and family will readily attest.

In this age of short attention spans, information overload and instant gratification, we're ALL looking for the easy button: to change our habits, to improve our lives, to add to our knowledge and expertise, to lose weight or to find our soul mate. The simple truth is that there ISN'T one. All of these things are obviously possible, and not overly difficult or complicated to achieve, but they don't happen by magic, or by pressing a simple button. What they do require is focused and determined effort and action on our parts. It helps to have a clear understanding of the WHY in what we want and need to learn or change, so that we can realistically decide and evaluate if a program is going to provide that answer, or at least send us down the correct path towards our ultimate goal(s).

I have rightly been described as being an information sponge and have always been a big proponent of investing in one's personal self-education, as well as furthering your professional education and skills. I have received substantial benefits from this practice, but I've also experienced just as many disappointments in my efforts, and substantial expenditures. This has occurred mostly when I've tried to seek in others, or their products, what I wanted to see in them, as opposed to what was actually there or the benefit(s) they would realistically provide to me (aka Shiny Object Syndrome).

The problem with this type of behavior, while it may be well-meaning and good intentioned, is that it can cause the following likely negative outcomes:

1. It can provide you with a false sense of security.

2. It can cause you to become uncertain and make you feel *inadequate*.

3. It can cause you to feel overwhelmed and more confused.

4. It can also cause you to become more indecisive.

5. It can cause you to always be chasing the next magic pill, or solution, and never focusing on finishing and mastering the program(s) that you already own (a perpetual dog chasing his own tail).

In the end, I would still likely make all of the investments that I've made in the past, and will continue to so invest in the future, but I will do so with the understanding and knowledge that the mere act of purchase does not constitute an education. Action is always necessary for growth.

My suggestion to you is to finish and master one program at a time, before you're distracted by the next flashy, wiz-bang, shiny object that's sure to come along. You already have enough information at your fingertips right now for you to be successful. Take action with the techniques and lessons taught and then move on to the next.

Do *YOU* have biz training programs collecting dust on your computer and/or your book shelves? (C'mon, be honest with yourself!) Keep in mind that reading books, watching videos, and/or listening to audios alone WILL NOT change the circumstances of your life or your business. *You MUST ACT upon what you have learned to get results.* Education is the first step toward biz success, but ACTION is the second step - and the sometimes harsh reality is that NOTHING HAPPENS WITHOUT IT! And so I strongly encourage you to take action again, and again, and again!

> *"The man who doesn't read good books has no advantage over the man who can't read them."* - Mark Twain

Collectively putting these pieces together has benefitted me greatly over the course of my entrepreneurial journey. Far too often in life we try to reinvent the wheel, so to speak, which can be the cause of much heartache, financial loss, and a feeling of helplessness, which in turn can lead to the entrepreneur giving up.

I have had many forms of mentors and coaches over the course of this journey, and the information that I have supplied in this chapter and all of the contributions to this book can help lead you on your journey. I can't highly enough recommend (again) to go find your coach, or mentor!

> *"The world does not pay people for that which they 'know', it pays them for what they do, or induce others to do."* – Napoleon Hill

---

To Contact Michael:

Email: Michael@underwearentrepreneur.com

Website: www.underwearentrepreneur.com

Magazine: www.underwearentrepreneurmag.com

Naomi Douglas

Naomi Douglas is a Divorce Coach, Marriage Coach, and Family Mediator. She helps individuals and couples through all stages of marriage, divorce and co-parenting.

Naomi works internationally via phone and Skype. She also works face to face when that is appropriate.

Naomi has a background in relationship counseling, mediation, social work and early childhood education. She is registered as an FDRP with the Attorney General of Australia.

She brings a compassion and wisdom to her work that allows her clients to experience accelerated growth and profound changes over short periods of time.

Naomi grew up in New York City and resides in Australia. She has three children.

Facing Divorce and Other Crises: how to allow life to transform you

By Naomi Douglas

When our life is over, what are we left with?

I have no authority with which to answer that question; I ask it because I think that sometimes the important thing is asking the right questions. I personally believe that we are left with the growth that our soul has made throughout our life. My impression from observation is that all of life is an evolution. I think we are here to grow; we are here to evolve.

Life is often challenging. Relationships are certainly challenging, and so is change. Few things are more challenging than divorce. Divorce is an area I specialize in, along with marriage reconciliation.

The stakes are high during divorce. There is a lot that can be won or lost; people's lives are dramatically altered. A lot of people get hurt during divorce. Many children are deeply hurt. I am convinced that our society as a whole is greatly damaged by the suffering that many adults and children experience during divorce. I am also convinced that there is a great deal that can be done about this. This is a problem that, to a large extent, can be solved.

By definition, the issues that plagued a marriage remain unresolved throughout a divorce; divorce is the result of unresolved problems.

Marriage problems are always based on our deepest issues and most difficult emotions. Marriage is a place where these issues and emotions need to be healed and transformed. When this does not happen, the result is either a painfully unhappy marriage or a divorce.

Faced with what frequently seems the impossible task of saving a marriage, divorce appears to be the only solution. But divorce itself is a mammoth undertaking and is plagued by emotions which, far from diminishing, often escalate.

During divorce there are big questions to answer, such as who gets what and what happens to the children, and so this fragile and volatile personal tragedy often lands in a legal system which is not designed to heal people but is designed to pit them against each other in an adversarial battle which can reach epic proportions.

My stand is for healing, and personal development. I help people to triumph in the face of adversity by discovering their capacity to learn and to grow. This protects families from conflicts that cause widespread damage to children and society as a whole.

Crisis (which divorce is one example of) is a change that is brought about by something significant that is unable to remain the same because of forces, both within and outside of ourselves, that will not allow it to do so. As this breakdown occurs, we are confronted with everything that holds us back and separates us from our innate potential. Because of the force involved in crisis, a great deal of growth becomes possible. We must find what it is that can regenerate within us, because otherwise we are bound to identify only with what is being destroyed. In order to harness our capacity to regenerate, we need to understand our inner natures better.

The undeveloped aspects of ourselves that drive unwanted behavior and produce unwanted results in our lives are the youngest and most sensitive parts of ourselves. We make the mistake of assuming that upon reaching adulthood, we are 'grown up.' I think there is a continuum, with parts of ourselves developing and maturing much faster than other parts. If you pay close attention to your internal world, when you are upset or struggling with something, you will probably find that the feelings you are experiencing have a very young quality to them - as if it is a small child who is feeling them. That hurt young child still exists and plays a significant role in our adult lives. That hurt young child is in need of healing.

I have a working theory that the parts of ourselves that are the slowest to develop (which hence makes them so problematic and unappealing to us), are in fact, the parts of ourselves that hold the majority of our potential and our greatness. My guess is that these parts are the slowest to develop because they are the most sensitive, and hence the most vulnerable. And it is this sensitivity that potentially is the richest source of creativity, inspiration, individuality and talent.

Bruce Perry, in discussing trauma work with children, explains that it is not necessary for us to understand psychology to heal these children. Young children have the capacity to heal simply by having a person in their lives who pays them loving attention. I think the same applies to the hurt childlike parts of our selves. If we understand these wounded parts of self to be small and fragile children who are paralyzed by painful emotions, we can discover how to heal, and we can engage in a dynamic 'growing up' process.

Often my clients are parents of young children. Divorcing parents sometimes feel that it is difficult to cope with everything they are going through emotionally while at the same time trying to be good parents. I say that our children hold the keys to our healing. They are the ones that show us how to be compassionate and present and kind to the young and fragile parts of ourselves. If we can translate what we do so naturally as parents to our own 'inner children' we can tap into a very healing experience. Think of the hurt inner child as a sibling to your own children. When your children are enjoying happy times such as bedtime stories, cuddles and games, make a little mental image of your younger self joining in. Rather than bombard our children with adult problems, divorce is a time to immerse ourselves in the wonder of our children's childhoods, for their sakes *as well as our own*.

A marriage breakdown is one of the most difficult challenges that anyone can face. When a marriage breaks down, we lose the person who was our lover, partner and best friend. Even if the relationship was an unhappy one it's end represents the loss of the dreams we once had. On top of that, the most important aspects of our life change in ways that shake us to our core. We lose time with our children, we lose financial resources we often lose our home. A breakup is an ordeal that involves intense emotions that involve our most complex psychological issues. While we are in the throes of all of this, we divide property and the care of our children. At a time when we are the least capable of thinking clearly we are making some of the biggest decisions of our lives.

We often add to the mix lawyers, who either wittingly or unwittingly turn our anguish and ailing psyches into a battlefield. The relationship between ex-partners, already broken and bleeding, can descend quickly in the hands of these experts of the adversarial legal system in an atmosphere of bitterness and resentment of the highest order. The result of all this is that large percentages of a family's net worth is spent on legal fees while children become the casualties of a family war zone. And rather than healing the gaping wounds left from the severed relationship, the ex husband and wife are left with more hurt and more problems than they ever imagined they would face in their lifetime.

When my son was a toddler, I was drawn to a photo on the front page of the Guardian. It was of a two year old boy sitting alone on a barren patch of ground in a refuge camp of a war torn country. He had lost his parents in that war. I was overwhelmed by the pain I felt for this poor child. He reminded me of my little boy, but this boy was alone and I could not help him. I took a walk to try to come to terms with my feelings. All I could think was that war causes unbelievable hurt and that if I contributed in any way to a lack of peace on our planet then I must be sure to correct that. I did the only thing I felt I could do for this little boy. I made a pledge that I would strive to never in my actions contribute in any way to war. I would overcome any aspect of myself that hindered me from bringing peace into the world.

Perhaps ironically, some ten years later I became, much to my shock and horror, embroiled in a bitter divorce that damaged all members of my family. I do not know how much of this was fate, but I do know that my true calling is to bring healing to this very troubled landscape of human affairs.

The question of whether a marriage should indeed end is an important one, and is individual. For some people the only healthy choice is to end a relationship. For many, it is not the relationship per say thAT is the problem, it is the individuals' inability to respond productively to the challenges that relationship brings up. I love when I bring broken couples back together, which sometimes happens, even if they have come to me for help in planning their divorce. The reason for the change is that often marriages end not because they cannot endure, but because those involved have not understood correctly what is wrong and do not have the skills or guidance to fix the problem.

Every divorce represents a world of pain, which is a dangerous place for children, as the two people who they need and love the most become torn apart, often violently. The lawyers and the judges may try to help but they often lead families onto battlefields which are not equipped for healing and have no facility for vulnerability. During such cataclysmic times, families need a chance to stabilize, to regroup, to heal and come to terms with the changes they are faced with. They need child friendly environments to adjust and develop new family structures.

Crises are intense opportunities to grow, if only people have access to the knowledge and tools necessary to make this possible. That is why, though legal professionals are usually a necessary part of a divorce, they should be understood to play only a very specific part in the overall proceedings. An essential component is the professional who can protect their clients from the incredible financial and emotional costs of a high conflict divorce and who is able to guide those clients through a period of accelerated personal development. This is the role I play as a divorce coach.

There is not enough room in this chapter to cover the complexities of divorce or the many essential skills involved in parenting before, during and after divorce. Instead, I would like to speak about an emotion that my clients often struggle with. That emotion is regret, and it is an emotion that has captured my imagination.

In my book, *Persephone's Return: a woman returns from the underworld guided by ancient myth and the internet*, I describe a process I developed to work with regret which I call *The Rescue Mission*. The theory behind The Rescue Mission is that regret is a symptom of something we need to correct in present time. We tend to think of regret as a rather useless feeling because it always relates to the past, and the past is of course something that we cannot change. I have come to believe that the reason we feel regret is that there is something significant about our past that has bearing on our present, and indeed our future.

I believe that our regrets highlight times in our lives when we failed to access important parts of ourselves that were needed to bring about desirable results. I think the reason these past experiences play on our minds is that those aspects are still needed in our present in order to actualize the future we are yearning for. I have discovered that if we go back to the part of our past that invokes a strong feeling of regret, we can work with that experience by reimagining our story into something that we wish had happened. In doing so we access the lost parts of selves that we so badly required then, and which we truly need in the present. This is why I call the process the 'Rescue Mission.' We are literally rescuing lost parts of our self.

A young separated couple came to me to work out a care arrangement for their baby. Their marriage had fallen apart around the time of the child's birth. I worked with both parents to sort out their feelings and communicate with each other better. Through the process, I was able to help them to see that their marriage could be saved. There was not something irreparable in their marriage; there was a lack of understanding and skill when it came to addressing their problems. I taught them how to work with their relationship problems in a new way. This process was a fairly big one, because a lot of damage had been done during the breakup. The wife, particularly felt unable to show up for her husband because of the pain that she had experienced. I had been coaching her for a while on what it would look like if she brought her power into the relationship. She remained wary and reluctant to do so because she didn't want to be hurt again.

During this time, she confided in me that a few years earlier, they had aborted a baby. She felt very ashamed about this and felt that decision could not be justified. I suggested we do a Rescue Mission. I asked her to go back to the time when the two of them decided to have an abortion. In her Rescue Mission she wanted them to decide to have the baby. I asked her what it would have taken for that to happen. She thought about it and said she would have had to be stronger. She would have had to tell him that she was confident that they could make it work. She thought about who she would have had to be to do this. She saw that she had needed to feel more confident in herself, that she had needed to be more powerful. Then she was quiet. I could almost hear her brain while it contemplated this revelation. "This is how I need to be now with Steve, isn't it?" she asked. I knew that this is exactly what I had been trying to coach her to do in her relationship but I did not immediately say this. I wanted her to get this on her own. "I think," I said gently, "you will find that this would relate to many aspects of your life." "But," she said with a new strength in her voice, "this is really how I need to show up for Steve now, isn't it?" As she considered what a great loss it was to have aborted their first child, she was now also seeing that she might lose the chance of reconciling with Steve if she did not now learn the lesson of finding her confidence and showing up in her power.

When we become aware of the hurt fragile parts of ourselves, we have the opportunity to care for them as kindly and lovingly as any parent cares for their babies. When we address the parts of our past that still cause us concern, we have the ability to harness our imaginative power and make something right that up until this point has not been. There is always the possibility of healing, and of growing into our potential. My point is, it is never too late to become who we truly are.

To Contact Naomi:

Naomi Douglas

www.NaomiDouglas.com.au

+61421421757

naomi@NaomiDouglas.com.au

Reverend Susan (Sue) Henley

Reverend Sue provides spiritual grief counseling that aids healing after loss of a loved one, loss of a career, home, or a number of other difficult and unpredictable life circumstances. She also provides spiritual life counseling, inspiring and teaching clients to find harmony and peace be it at home, work, or within relationships.

Reverend Sue is a certified Spiritual Counselor, a Reiki Master, and an ordained Spiritual Peace Minister with The Beloved Community and Universal Life Church. With more than a decade of experience, she performs weddings, baptisms, and funerals in her native state of Arizona. She is also the author of an autobiographical novel, *Because of Sean*, and a work of fiction, *Sara, Beyond the Veil: A Spiritual Look at Dementia*.

Reverend Sue is a valuable asset to her community as she is dedicated to her clients and their wellbeing, and embodies a passion for educating others on the skills essential to the discovery and sustainment of a full and happy life.

Holistic House Calls, LLC - Founding Member

American Holistic Medical Association (AHMA) - Certified Practitioner and Member

Arizona Fiduciaries Association - Affiliate Member

Dementia Therapy Specialists - Member

Just Breathe

By Rev. Susan J. Henley

We've all heard it. Just Breathe. Why not try it now. Take a deep breath. Breathe deeply and imagine you are floating, floating away from all cares and concerns of your everyday existence. Imagine you are enveloped in loving arms. There is silence and peace while being held in the arms of pure love.

The power of the unseen force of air is shown to us every day. The wind moves and trees bend, a sail boat glides on the water, clouds drift in the sky. What is this magical force that moves upon the earth and sustains us, giving us life, energy and attention? Air sustains our life and we cannot exist without it. It affects how you live, work, eat, sleep and play. Even as you sleep you are breathing. Breathe in this amazing energy and you will feed your body. Breathing in this life force energy from Heaven will feed your soul.

So how do we feed our soul? Surely we can imagine the air that sustains our bodies. That is simple. But feeding our soul with heavenly air? Well, that could be considered impossible for some or a challenge for others.

First, we must understand that we are all connected to each other in some way. This connection is so strong that when one act of kindness or one act of aggression is created, the entire world is affected. Dr. Masaru Emoto demonstrated how water molecules responded to words, music, pictures and video. His research provided us with insight as to how water reacts to what we focus on. Air consists of molecules as well. The same energy that Dr. Emoto demonstrated when focusing on an emotion, also affects air. If air is everywhere, and we focus on peace, then we spread peace everywhere. If we focus on destruction, we spread destruction.

As humans, we are all capable of great imagination. We do it every moment of every day. Our minds are a continuous flow of thoughts that either creates peace, joy and love, or sadness, pain and despair. When we take a deep breath and focus, just for a moment, on quieting our minds our bodies respond. And our blood pressure and heart rates are lowered. Deep breathing is an automatic stress reliever.

When we are in difficult emotional situations, we tend to hold our breath. If you will, imagine watching a very intense movie. There is a chase scene where a car is careening out of control through a crowded street. As we focus on the car and the ensuing rampage, we automatically take in short breaths, waiting for the outcome. While this may be an exciting entertainment option, in reality what are we focusing on? We have chosen to escape our everyday existence by watching movies that grasp our attention and excite us. In this amazing age of information and technology, many of us have become numb to the violence in our everyday society. We see outrageous acts by people and judge them while not standing in their shoes or even considering what might have brought them to act in the manner that they did. We have become numb to the 20 second blip on the news of some traumatic altercation between two people that affects everyone, not just those who participated in the action. It seems at times that we are helpless to make any change at all. And in the meantime we hold our breath.

In the alternative, we can sit quietly by the ocean, lake or stream and take in the essence of peace that is found within nature. By observation of the flow of the water, the sound of the birds, the feeling of the air gently touching our skin, our blood pressure and heart rate are lowered and we automatically take a deep breath. Focusing on the peace and quiet of the moment will change our energy and how we relate to the world around us. Even for a few minutes. If we are not able to leave our homes, we can choose to listen to recorded sounds of these peaceful stimulations and sit with our eyes closed, imagining that we are sitting on that beach, shore or by a brook.

Mindful Breathing.

Mindful breathing is the direct focus on breathing, with little to no outside distractions. When you begin to focus on your breathing you notice how your mind will jump from one topic to another. It helps us understand how our busy our minds actually are. When we focus, we can then bring our attention back to our breathing and assist in the slowing of the chatter of the mind. Focusing on breathing helps to reduce stress and has a positive effect on your wellbeing.

I've counseled people who say, "I'm so lost. I feel like I can't find my way home. Where is that place?" One way to find the answers to these is to practice mindful breathing. Let's take a look at what a typical day is for you and ask yourself these questions:

1. What is my routine in the morning?

2. If I am employed, how much time do I give myself before I begin the process of going to work?

3. If I commute to work, what do I listen to (if driving) or what am I reading (if taking public transportation)?

4. Once I arrive at work (whether it be in the home office or to the place of employment), what is the first thing I do?

5. Throughout my day, where is my attention? Is it on work, fellow employees, those around me and what they are doing or saying?

6. What is my return to home like? Once I get there, what do I focus on?

7. Now that the day is over, what is my routine for going to bed?

The answers to these questions will help you to become aware of what you are focusing (or not focusing) on.

Our work week has become a routine, right down to the time we leave for work, the route we take, the lunch we eat, who we eat it with or eating lunch alone, what we eat, how we drive home, etc. Our robot-like behavior has put us in a state of unawareness. At no time during that routine, do we mindfully breathe.

What if you decided that today was going to be different. What if you got up 5 minutes earlier every day and took those 5 minutes to mindfully breathe? You can begin right now where you are. Turn off the television, the radio, the computer game, and any outside distractions. Sit in a comfortable position. There are no rules about how you are sitting or even when you take your 5 minutes. You do not need to sit like a Buddhist Monk to accomplish mindful breathing. If you choose to lie down, there is a possibility that you will fall asleep. If it is time for bed, or you have the time to nap, then by all means, lay down. If you are sitting on a crowded bus, train or airplane, just do the best you can.

Let us begin. Close your eyes and take in a slow deep breath through your nose. Breathe out through your mouth and as you do this say the number "one." Good. Now, take in another breath and breathe out while saying "two." Continue with this until you reach the number 15. If you can't make it to 15, then try 10. If not 10 then try 5. Remove as much air as you can on the out-breath and breathe in as much as you can on the in-breath. Each time you should be able to accomplish bigger breaths.

Now that you have practiced, you can begin to add a thought with each in-breath. Why not focus on the word Peace. Breathe in Peace; breathe out the number "one." And so on and so on.

You are now on the road to great things. As you do this simple breathing exercise, you lower your blood pressure and lower the blood pressure of the world. Remember what happens to water molecules when we focus on a particular emotion? You are creating an effect on air molecules as well. The stronger you focus on the word Peace on the in-breath, the stronger it will be on the out-breath.

Congratulations. You've done it. You have taken the first step towards healing yourself and being part of something grand. You are now what is considered being in the "present moment." Not thinking of the past or the future, but only of the moment of your breath. And in reality, this is all there really is.

It is important to realize that there is nothing we can do about the past and focusing on it only brings about stress. You can, however, look back and learn from it. You can choose not to make the mistakes again because you have learned the lesson that the past shows you. Or, you can choose to make the same mistakes over and over and not move forward at all. But what would be the point in that?

Alternatively, we cannot control the future. We can prepare for it and hope for a bright future, but can we really control it? No. We can, however, create a vision of the future that holds bright and new beginnings for ourselves and our loved ones. This is called "holding space." You can do this while mindfully breathing. In your mind, place yourself in that new home or new job. See your children succeeding and spreading joy and peace wherever they go. And remember to breathe while doing this.

<u>Creating a sacred space.</u>

Many religions have a church and in this church there usually is an altar, or a place where the clergy stands and conducts the service. This is considered a "sacred space." You can create a sacred space in your home or office, or your back yard or at a park. A sacred space is different for everyone. If you enjoy looking at icons (statutes or photos) then I would suggest that you gather these items and place them where they won't be disturbed. You can choose from many different religions or one specific that feels right for you. If candles resonate with you, put them in the area and make the place holy for you.

I have a shelf in my home with two Native American women that have their arms reaching to the sky, three candles that represent the Trinity, photos of family and those who are in need or that I wish to keep safe, pictures of Holy people and various crystals. You might call it the cornucopia of religion. While I don't follow any specific religion, I feel great peace while looking at these particular items.

You can create this sacred space just for you or any of your family members that are supportive of what you are creating. Working together with family is a great way to create a peaceful area in your home. If, however, your family does not agree with your space, then you should claim it for yourself.

Light your candles, play quiet music that resonates with you and practice the mindful breathing exercises above. When you do this at least once a day, you are giving yourself a gift of peace. When you do it twice a day, you are giving yourself the gift of improved health. As you extend the time that you practice mindful breathing, your gift to yourself becomes greater; so your peace of mind and good health grow. What a wonderful way to start and end your day. Practice holding space for whatever you would like to see change in your life or that of your friends and family. Visualize the new beginning, breathe it in and breathe it out. Hear the sounds of the vision such as the wind, or music, and smell the grass or flowers that you see. Use your senses to create a sacred space in your heart.

Health Benefits of Mindful Breathing.

Continued or chronic stress brings about heart disease, anxiety, depression, and a larger variety of other health disorders. We are stressed about so many things such as paying the bills, what others think of us, our clothes and our cars. Large life events are obvious stressors, but if we really pay attention to how much we stress on the seemingly little things, we can see how much wear and tear our minds and bodies cannot handle. Mindful breathing assists in relieving stress, therefore the practice of mindful breathing is a sure way to promote wellbeing in your mind and ultimately your body will respond. It can assist you in improving memory and concentration, your emotional wellbeing and overall outlook on life.

When you are confronted with life altering decisions, practice mindful breathing. Many times the answers for your situation will come to you once you have quieted the chatter in your mind. If you are facing a move or changing jobs, focusing on your breathing allows the answers to come. When you are feeling overwhelmed by life, mindful breathing will help. Some examples of continuous or chronic stressors are:

> 1. Your job creates stress because you are asked to continuously multitask and have difficulty in being able to complete one project;

2. The drive to/from work took longer than anticipated and traffic was a real bear;

3. Once you are finally home, your wife/husband and children require most of your attention;

4. These constant stressors leave you feeling unenthusiastic about even getting up in the morning. It's easier to sit in front of the television after everyone is fed and in bed, if you have children, than to do much else.

In India, breath work called *pranayama* is a regular part of yoga practice. Yoga practitioners have used *pranayama*, which literally means control of the life force, as a tool for affecting both the mind and body for thousands of years. Often when I do a workshop or speaking engagement, I begin with asking everyone to take a deep breath. It creates a calming affect for everyone in the room, including myself. If we are to improve our lives and those of us around us, we first must choose something that is easy and very rewarding. Mindful breathing is a simple form of creating improvement in our lives.

Remember, if you are unhappy with any aspect of your life, mindful breathing will benefit you. No matter what your situation is, if you breathe in the breath of life, your life will improve. Or if you hold your breath, you will stay exactly where you are.

Continue to be the seeker until you arrive at your destination. You may not know for certain what that destination is, but as you travel along this highway of life, just breath.

Just Breathe

To contact Rev. Henley:

Website: www.revsusanhenley.com

Email: revsusanhenley@gmail.com

Sandi Mitchell

Sandi Mitchell is President and CEO of APEX Leadership Coaching, a firm dedicated to both people and profitability through intentional emphasis on leadership, negotiation, and emotional intelligence for extraordinary leaders. Sandi knows leadership requires more than simply having followers. Her passion is working with high-achieving leaders who want to transition from leading followers to leading leaders.

Sandi works with leaders from small businesses to major corporations to help improve and/or accelerate in areas such as: leadership presence and capability, senior team alignment, strategic planning, emotionally intelligent negotiations, and employee engagement. Her approach utilizes hands-on experiential learning, resulting in the highest impact and results through sustainable, long-term productivity improvements.

Sandi is certified as an executive coach who created and uses the APEX Leadership System™ – Awareness. Performance. Excellence. Xtraordinary. Leadership. She also specializes in emotionally intelligent negotiations through her EQ Negotiation™ program. Sandi is an international speaker and executive coach who connects to audiences, inspiring and motivating to reach even higher. She coaches exceptional people to be leaders AND leader makers. Sandi is The Inner Genius Coach™.

Strengthening Your Inner Genius

By Sandi Mitchell

Imagine yourself as a gladiator in the middle of a Roman arena ready to fight for your life. Thousands of people in the stands are and booing you, yelling that you're worthless, you're a loser. Then in the midst of the overwhelming chaos you hear one voice – the voice of your coach – saying you were made for this moment. You stand tall and face your challenge with strength, boldness and courage.

2000 years later and that scene with you in the middle of the screaming naysayers (your Inner Critics) and the one positive coach (your Inner Genius) is replaying in your mind. Who are you listening to – your Inner Critics or your Inner Genius?

I realized I am the one inflicting most of the hurtful words I hear. I used to say, "How could I be so stupid?", "I'm never good enough, it's hopeless." or "Why did I say that?" We sabotage ourselves with our own words. These come from our Inner Critics.

The Inner Critics are the voices we hear telling us we're not good enough, not strong enough, not smart enough, and on and on and on. The original purpose of the Inner Critics is to protect us from harm, embarrassment, or pity. It accomplishes this by wanting us to stay small and safe. Our Inner Critics don't know the difference between us being robbed at gunpoint or being promoted to a great job. Intellectually, we know the latter brings success, however, our Inner Critics view both as threats to our comfort and safety.

The Inner Genius's job is to propel us to our greatness. It works hard to overcome the loud negative voices of our Inner Critics. Frustratingly, unless you have honed your mind to hear it, you will likely only hear its whispers. Think of the Roman arena. That clear voice of the coach is your Inner Genius, guiding you past the destructive nature of your Inner Critics.

Here is a story of how one of my Inner Critics was born. My father travelled a lot when I was young and it was always exciting when he was expected home. My mother made sure each of us kids and the house were all clean and perfect. Everything was the epitome of sparkle, shine, and happiness when Dad came home.

Most of the time Dad was excited to see us. But there were times he would come home exhausted from his travels and we would be sent outside so Dad could get some peace and quiet. As the oldest and most mischievous of the three sisters, I assumed the reason he came home unhappy was due to whatever trouble I had gotten into before he came home.

I made a promise to myself to do everything possible to make him proud of me. I believed *that* would make him happy (translation: Dad would play with us). That moment created one of my biggest Inner Critics – my achievement earns love.

This Inner Critic (I call it the General Manager of the Universe) says I have to be the best or I'm nothing. When I fail, this Inner Critic says "See, I told you, you're just not good enough, you'll never be good enough." Its voice can easily drown out my Inner Genius.

Children lack the maturity and perspective to comprehend their experiences. Like most children, I did my best to make sense of my world. I believed my behavior dictated how much my dad loved me. It never occurred to me that my behavior had no bearing on his unconditional love for me. Without realizing it, I created an Inner

Critic that would pester me for decades. My Inner Critic pushed me to be the best – at sports, at school, or getting the next promotion. I was achieving so much I didn't take time to enjoy the celebrations of my achievements. I was always looking past to the next goal, the next accomplishment.

We get what we focus on the most. If we focus on what our Inner Critics' say, then we will see only negativity. If we focus on what our Inner Genius says, then we see more opportunities. It's as simple as that. Really.

Here are six steps to help you shift from listening to your Inner Critics to listening to your Inner Genius significantly more of the time. I call it the GENIUS plan. G.E.N.I.U.S. is an acronym for Gratitude, Exploring, Nourishing, Imagining, Uniqueness and Serving.

GRATITUDE: A 2013 study said only 13% of employees globally engage at work. This indicates that only one in eight workers commits to the job and makes positive contributions. Consider how that attitude of disengagement, negativity, and apathy affects people not only at work, but in their home and social lives as well. Most are listening to their Inner Critics.

An attitude of gratitude changes people's lives. How do you bring more gratitude into your life? One way is by practicing gratitude exercises – reminding ourselves where we have been at our best, felt gratitude, when we have listened to our Inner Genius and, thus, succeeded.

Here are three of many simple gratitude exercises that can help increase thankfulness, appreciation, and gratitude in your life.

- Thank you notes. When did you last sit down and write a thank you note? Not email, or text, but a handwritten note? Write a letter to someone who positively influenced your life

– a teacher, a mentor, family member, anyone who has helped you along the way. Be specific about what they did and how it affected you. Mail it, or better yet, hand-deliver it.

- Gratitude Lookout. Choose a day to find people to thank. Actively watch for ways to thank others for their kindness, helpfulness, or consideration. Be generous with your thanks!

- Put Things in Perspective. When things go wrong, use the power of gratitude to change your perception. Our brains are wired to answer questions. When faced with adversity, ask yourself the following questions:

    o What is good about this?

    o How can I benefit from this?

    o What can I learn from this?

    o What can I feel grateful for in this situation?

    o What is the opportunity here?

One recent study explains people who practice gratitude are more likely to reach their goals, enjoy improved health, sleep better, gain more energy, have a stronger love life, support others more, and have increased likability.

It takes 21 days to create a habit. Research shows it takes 66 days for a habit to permeate your subconscious so you can do it without thinking about it (i.e., tying your shoe). Practice gratitude for the next 66 days and see how it changes your life and the lives of those around you.

EXPLORING: Our brains are lazy. You could call it efficient, too. They are naturally wired to see patterns in the world around us and then pushes what it can into those known patterns. Then the subconscious brain can deal with the event rather than the conscious brain. For example, how many times have you driven to or from home and you don't actually remember how you got there. Your conscious brain was thinking about other things while your subconscious brain was driving. Scary!

The vast majority of our subconscious brain focuses on the patterns, the habits, the rules our Inner Critics enforce. The subconscious brain believes what we tell it, and then it seeks self-fulfilling prophecies. For example, If I say I don't believe I'm a good enough leader to get that next promotion, my brain will take everything I have done and do wrong, whether real or perceived, as an opportunity to prove to me I was right in my belief. So my Inner Critics then get to jump on the negative bandwagon and say "See, I didn't get promoted so it must be true I'm not a good enough leader." Our Inner Critics are sneaky that way!

The good news is that the brain just does what we train it to do. When we focus on our Inner Genius, our Inner Genius provides better and more creative decision-making options.

Three tools for exploring and expanding your Inner Genius.

- Passwords. One way to create a new pattern for our subconscious brain is to consistently repeat it – remember 66 days? For example, in the past I have used passwords such as "MBAin2oo2" – "H3althyM3" – "Wa!kingDai!y". Make your passwords into positive statements. What do you want to focus on in the next 66 days? Create an Inner Genius password for it.

- Rules. Explore your mind and uncover the rules your Inner Critic has created. For example, some of my clients had rules such as "when dad gets angry use humor to distract him," "never tell anyone what goes on behind closed doors," or "don't show vulnerability or incompetence." There are also rules such as don't cross the street without looking both ways, believe someone when they tell you who they are, and exercise keeps you healthy. By bringing the rule forward to your conscious brain, then you can determine if you want to keep it, change it, or eliminate it for a new, more Inner Genius inspired rule.

- Values. Search on the Internet for "values lists" and choose the values that most resonate with you. Prioritize your top five. Why are these important to you? Values come from fear or love. You are afraid of losing something (security) or love the way you feel having it (family). How do your values align with the way you live your life, your business, or the people in your life? When dissonance exists in our lives, it can typically be traced back to a conflict with one of our core values. Having your values aligned with your work and life encourages a happier you.

NOURISHING: We need to nourish ourselves – and our brains!

John Maxwell, leadership expert, says, "The unfortunate truth is that most people are desperate for encouragement (including ourselves!)... become a nurturer to them because people are influenced by those who make them feel the best about themselves." Our brain works 24/7 multitasking billions of details while ensuring our bodies work for decades. It keeps the brain thinking, heart pumping, lungs breathing, eyes seeing, ears hearing, bones and muscles in place, and billions of other activities. Be grateful for your brain. Take care of it.

Three ways to nourish your brain are:

- Relief – I call this Intentional Rejuvenation. The brain must be able to wind down and relax. Think about an athlete in training. They work out different muscle groups at different times so they can rest and recover quickly. Rest takes effort – beyond just sleeping in on the weekend hoping to make up for all the late nights during the week. We need intentional disconnecting. Go offline a couple of days to eliminate information overload.

- Exercise – Use your brain or lose it – so stimulate it! Games, puzzles, learning musical instruments, new languages, dancing – new and difficult activities that force you to think and problem solve will build and preserve your brain for years. Physical exercise is as important as mental exercise in the longevity of a healthy brain. Nourish your brain – learn, read, grow. Learning something new and interesting actually stimulates the same pleasure sensors in our brain that loves chocolate, drugs, and love. Isn't learning healthier than drugs?

- Nutrition – We are what we eat – you have probably heard before. It's true. 25% of our body's energy goes to maintaining our brain. With the war going on in your brain, who wins with your current diet? Will it be the Inner Critics – "relax, it's just your birthday, you deserve the sugar crash nap you'll get afterwards?" Or will it be the Inner Genius – "let's have that delicious fruit and remain clear-minded, sharp and focused?"

IMAGINING: Our brains are so powerful that our imagination can manifest itself into reality. For years, athletes have used visioning to see themselves making the free throw, or the touchdown, or hitting the ball into the centerfield stands. Zig Ziglar tells a story of a Vietnam prisoner of war who realized one way to stay sane during his years in camp was by daily playing a mental game of golf on the course by his home. He could even imagine the individual blades of grass bending when he put his ball on the tee. When he finally made it back home, he found he had knocked 20 strokes off his average. Your mind has the power to influence the outcome of whatever you try to do. Imagining cannot do it alone, though – you must still put in the work to hone your talents and put the habits in place for achieving success.

To strengthen your Inner Genius, imagine the future you want as your Ideal Self – the true you. The "you" your Inner Genius sees. Remember the Roman arena – you were made for this moment! That is your Ideal Self. The clearer your vision is for your future, being specific in describing the images enables your Inner Genius to more easily overcome the Inner Critic voices. Our imagination is powerful. Use it for your good.

Here are four questions to help you begin the imagining process:

- If your life were perfect and your dreams come true, what would your life and work be like in 10 years?

- What kind of person would you love to be? (What are the values most important to you – such as, accomplishment, creativity, independence, influence, recognition?)

- Who helped you the most in becoming who you are or get to where you are?

- If you won 50 million after tax in the lottery, how would your life or work change?

Gandhi said, "Your beliefs become your thoughts, your thoughts become your words, your words become your actions, your actions become your habits, your habits become your values, your values become your destiny." What do you want your destiny to be? Let your Inner Genius help you imagine what your Ideal Self looks like.

UNIQUENESS: We are all unique and yet most of us refuse to believe it. We assume because something is easy for us, it must be easy for others. So we think we're not unique. However, because of the experiences we have had, the people in our lives, the books we have read, the thoughts and feelings and actions we have had, we do have a unique way of looking at life. It is our obligation to share our uniqueness.

The dictionary describes unique as meaning, "without equal, incomparable, unequalled, unmatched, being the only one of a particular type, and very remarkable."

Most of us spend our childhood trying to be like the others around us and yet we feel unlike anyone around us. So our Inner Critics got the opportunity to run wild!

Now that you have transitioned from childhood to adulthood – you get to recognize your uniqueness, your individuality, your incomparability. How wonderful would it be if the children you know were consistently reminded of their uniqueness?

Look at the people who have understood and used their individuality to the benefit of the world:

- Malala Yousafzai – a teenaged girl from Pakistan who overcame an attack from the Taliban and used her passion for learning to become a global activist for education.

The Change 3

- Seth Godin – a marketing expert who changed the way we market with the concept of permission marketing versus traditional interruption advertising.

- Steve Jobs – a guru of iconoclastic thinking who let seemingly disparate things (a class in calligraphy, a stay at an ashram, and a friendship with a technical nerd, Steve Wozniak) come together in his mind to create Apple and change the face of technology.

- And so many more – Maya Angelou, Nelson Mandela, Margaret Thatcher, Gandhi, world leaders, humanitarians, and spiritual guides.

Each of them recognized and developed their uniqueness and strengths. By noticing and developing their uniqueness, our world has evolved as well. You don't have to change *the* world, but developing your strengths, your uniqueness can change *your* world, and in turn, those people around you. You impact people whether you want to or not. You get to choose – is your impact driven by your Inner Critics or your Inner Genius?

What is unique about you?

SERVING: When we live in negativity, we can't help but focus on ourselves – almost exclusively. When we focus exclusively on ourselves, we put on blinders or filters and can only see the small picture. When we remove the blinders or filters, we expand our perspective of the world – we focus on others, we grow in openness, we help others in their endeavors and help give voice to their Inner Genius.

Helping others floods our brains with epinephrine (gives us a sense of peacefulness, well-being, and calm) and testosterone (gives us energy for creativity). Helping literally energizes our brain and makes us feel better.

The whole notion of noticing people has become a big part of my life lately. Just by noticing, I see opportunities of service, have unexpected conversations that expand my thinking, and sometimes just sit with someone and enjoy the companionable silence.

When was the last time you really "noticed" someone? The next person you come in contact with, look closely enough see and notice the color of their eyes. Watch for someone who looks as if they could use help – an encouraging word, a ride somewhere, being there with a listening heart. Today, do one act of service for another person.

Remember, our Inner Critics can be overcome by strengthening our Inner Genius – through gratitude, exploring, nourishing, imagining, understanding your uniqueness, and serving others.

Now what? What are some ways your Inner Critic keeps you from achieving your goals? What are ways you can listen less to your Inner Critics and more to your Inner Genius this week?

If you are interested in finding out more about how to *Stop Your Inner Critic and Become an Extraordinary Leader,* or *Exploring Your Inner Genius*, learn more at InnerGeniusCoach.com.

In closing, I believe an obstacle to your Inner Genius and the life you have imagined can become one of two things:

1. It can become a stopping place for your Inner Critics to rail against the unfairness of it all, or

2. It can become a stepping stone into your greatness.

So the next time you come up against an obstacle, ask yourself, what greatness am I about to step into?

To our success!

Contact Info:

Sandi Mitchell, CPC, ACC, MBA

APEX Leadership Coaching, LLC

Awareness. Performance. Excellence. Xtraordinary. Leadership.

682.200.1412

Info@ApexLeadershipCoaching.com

ApexLeadershipCoaching.com

InnerGeniusCoach.com

www.linkedin.com/in/sandimitchell

https://www.facebook.com/sandi.mitchell.coaching

@CoachSandiM

References:

Gallup (2013). *State of the Global Workplace*.

Wood, Alex M., Maltby, John, Gillett, Raphael, Linley, P. Alex, Joseph, Stephen (August 2008). The role of gratitude in the development of social support, stress, and depression: Two longitudinal studies. *Journal of Research in Personality*.

Lally, P., van Jaarsveld, C. H. M., Potts, H. W. W., & Wardle, J. (2010). How are habits formed: Modeling habit formation in the real world. *European Journal of Social Psychology, 40,* 998-1009.

Maxwell, John and Dornan, Jim. *Becoming a Person of Influence: How to Positively Impact the Lives of Others*, 1997.

Ripollés, Pablo, Marco-Pallarés, Josep, Hielscher, Ulrike, Mestres-Missé, Anna, Tempelmann, Claus, Heinze, Hans-Jochen, Rodríguez-Fornells, Antoni, Noesselt, Toemme (2014). The Role of Reward in Word Learning and Its Implications for Language Acquisition. *Current Biology*.

http://www.collinsdictionary.com/dictionary/english/unique (accessed December 14, 2014).

Sonja-Sophie

Sonja-Sophie, born and raised in former East Germany, arrived in the US in 1994, at age 19. In 1996, she joined the US Army and was stationed in Italy and the US where she taught suicide prevention classes and pregnant soldier wellness programs.

Her upbringing in a communist country combined with her experiences in the Army give her a unique perspective and ability to understand people and the deep impact culture and traditions have on them, allowing her to effectively guide clients to success.

Her passion lies in inspiring women to develop a healthy body, mind and soul, gain inner peace and cultivate the courage to live extraordinary lives. She believes that in order to achieve greatness, it is critical to establish a winning mindset, focus on superb nutrition and follow a personalized exercise routine. Therefore she continues to study in all three areas.

Sonja-Sophie is a certified Personal Trainer, Health and Life Coach. She has worked with entrepreneurs, mothers, models, actresses and soldiers and is inspired by her clients' life transformations.

Food for Thought - Creating a Powerful Mindset

By Sonja-Sophie

You've heard it before: In order to change your life and create success you must change your thoughts. If you have tried this approach, you are well aware that this is much easier said than done. In fact, most of the people out there fail to accomplish this their entire lifetime and leave the planet without ever having lived their dreams. Don't let that be you!

Today, I want to share with you concepts that will enable you to effectively change your thoughts and gain true control over your mind, no matter how disorganized, unfocused or out of control your thoughts are right now. I am not talking about "positive thinking," a strategy that works only when you actually implement the concepts I am about to share with you first. They are the foundation on which you can build sustaining positive thought. Implement these concepts and watch them work wonders in your life. The beautiful thing is that you will be able to put into action most of what I am about to share as soon as you finish reading!

As I introduce these concepts to you, I will share short stories from my own life or my clients' experiences to show you how the implementation of these concepts can work in your life, too. Let's get started…

First I want to make clear that, in order to change your thoughts permanently to empower and inspire you, relying on willpower is a poor choice. The traditional concept of willpower is overrated, because it is based on motivation and emotions. Emotions come and go, as does willpower, leaving you feeling defeated, possibly depressed. In order to create lasting success, you must change your definition of willpower. When you define willpower as "having a powerful mind," strong, focused and ready to help you succeed, you can implement practices which help you strengthen your mind's power. The concepts I am revealing to you are all geared toward empowering your mind, body and soul and when they are implemented, your life is guaranteed to change in ways you cannot imagine today.

The creation of a powerful mind requires the mastery of five basic concepts:

1) Feeding Your Thought

2) Reclaiming Your Story

3) Practicing Radical Self Love

4) Getting to Know Your Self, Your Values and Strengths

Let me get straight to the purple miracle pill now, a concept called "Feeding your thought-positively." If you only take away one thing from what I am sharing, let it be this: You are what you eat – quite literally. Think about it – whatever you put into your mouth eventually becomes part of you in some way. Science has proven that food directly affects every single cell in your body, organs, ligaments, skin, your hormone household as well as your feelings, emotions and moods! Did you realize that the foods you ingest could actually make you depressed and moody? I realized that something was seriously wrong with me on the day my best friend told me about a nasty fight she'd had with her parents, when I caught myself repeating only one thought in my head: "Where can I get a snickers bar? Seriously, I need one right now." As hard as I tried to focus on what she was saying, it was to no avail. The need to satisfy my looming sugar craving had completely hijacked my brain. "I am addicted to sugar." I thought. During that time, I also experienced bouts of depression, often accompanied by a strong wish to leave this planet early. It never occurred to me then that many of my negative, self-distracting thoughts were a direct result of what I was eating.

Twenty years and countless trials and tribulations later, I have finally found a way out of the vicious cycle so many of us are experiencing and made it my mission to share with everyone how powerful the foods we eat affects not only our bodies, but our whole lives, and even our thought processes. I know of people who have been healed from depression by radically changing their diets, in fact I might say that I am one of them. Today it is almost funny how clearly I can point out the source of a "kind of depressing day" by checking in with my food diary.

Cleaning up your diet is the single most powerful action you can take in your life to enable you to gain superb control over your thoughts. Not doing so means constantly rowing against the stream, and will require tremendous amounts of energy on your part. How much do the pizza, chips and fries really mean to you? If you knew that giving up the junk food means getting rid of the junk thoughts in your head, could you make a decision that empowered you to truly create the life you dream of? Superb nutrition translates into a healthy, strong and resilient mind. My client, let's call her Lisa, struggled in her business. Her thoughts were scattered and her efforts unfocused and inconsistent. She was not happy with her weight and her self-esteem suffered. The crazy diets she had tried before left her feeling moody, unfocused and without energy to get her work done. I knew she'd love my program right then! In the following weeks, every phone conversation started with her saying: "I can't believe how much energy I have! And how clear I am thinking. No more clouds, all sharp! Do you think this has to do with what I am eating?" Of course! It had everything to do with the food. Today, her business has grown by leaps and bounds and she has become an inspiration to countless women across the world. She always had what it takes, and adopting a clean and healthy diet enabled her to gain control of her thoughts, which in turn allowed her to truly change her life. Cleaning up your diet the right way will empower you, leave you feeling younger, energetic and in charge of your future. Don't hesitate any longer and empower yourself today by establishing a healthy, nourishing way of eating. The benefits are countless and the real prize is your ability to build a life you love!

With your thoughts being fed in a positive way, you can move on to implementing the next concept I call "Reclaiming your story." Everyone goes through hardships, failures, embarrassments and all sorts of unpleasant or downright traumatic experiences. The way you deal with them determines if your thought processes become paralyzing or empowering. Again, you are not simply a bystander. You can take action to ensure that the events of your life become tools to cultivate a powerful mind. The basic premise of reclaiming your story is that you can take any negative experience and use it to your advantage simply by taking on a different view of what happened. Not by trying to forget what happened or minimize and disregard the effects it had on you, but by separating facts from emotions, and therefore diminishing its negative impact on your thought patterns and emotional realm. You then give the situation a new meaning; approach it with a different attitude. This is why two people being faced with the same situation can display extremely differing reactions. While one person will use the incident as an excuse for not taking charge of her life, the other will overcome and conquer her world, inspiring countless others in the process. Even the biggest tragedy can be turned it into a source of strength and inspiration. It is one of the most precious qualities humans possess. It is the essence of the human spirit. Clues to hidden stories are thoughts like: "I always do this," "This always happens to me," "I knew this would happen again." Disempowering stories keep you stuck in patterns and keep you from reaching the next level. When taking apart your own stories, you first write down what you feel happened, then extract the plain and simple facts of what happened, and lastly rewrite the story in a way that empowers you, or simply drop it for lack of significance. When you fill your mind with empowering stories and drop the ones no longer useful to you, the most daunting situations can become sources of great strength. Remember that new stories are created every day, so developing a practice that enables you to assess, re-write and drop a story in a matter of minutes can turn your life around in a very short time. Other practices such as Tapping (EFT) or going over the process with someone you trust can help you jumpstart the practice.

Let's move on to the next concept. This could be the most important of all, because when you master this one, implementing all others comes naturally. Extraordinary times require extraordinary measures. I'm asking you now to practice self-love in the most radical way you can stomach. You probably haven't been encouraged to love yourself much while growing up. There is definitely something wrong with our culture. You may have heard phrases like "Who do you think you are?" or "You think you're so important!" or "Do you think you're better than…?" directed at you after displaying innocent, but self-loving behavior during childhood. This can lead to believing that it is not appropriate to be gentle and caring with yourself. On top of that, you may have been encouraged to compete and out-do everyone. In a dog-eat-dog world, there's no place for love, period. Narcissism and conceitedness are not what I am talking about. Radical self-love is expressed every time you chose to take care of your body, mind and soul. Just as you are told on every major airline flight to put the oxygen mask on yourself first, and then assist others, realize that you cannot possibly take care of your loved ones effectively unless you learn to take care of yourself first. Since we live in a society that is not rooted in self-love, this means making decisions that can seem to be contradictory - like practicing less self-indulgence, or adopting inconvenient habits such as regular exercise, or spending less time with friends who encourage you to smoke or drink lots of alcohol when getting together. Your body happens to be the vehicle your soul is living in. You only have that one, and a person who practices radical self-love will ask constantly: Is this thing I am about to do an expression of respect, care and love for myself or others? Suddenly it becomes easier to leave the junk food on the table. Knowing the importance of your lymphatic system flushing out heavy metals and toxins, why would you chose to skip an opportunity to move around and let it do what it does to give you energy and vibrant skin? You only want the best for the ones you love. I want you to want the best for yourself, not the best looking, best-selling or most creatively advertised. In your heart you already know what is good for you. If you hear yourself saying things like: "I know I should (go to bed, drink less alcohol, eat more veggies, etc.), but I (insert excuse of your choice)," you are not acting from a place of radical self-love. Now don't start beating yourself up either. Forgiving yourself for your shortcomings is critical when learning to love your-self. Inner peace, empathy and a sense of "I am enough and I have enough," are the result of practicing self-love. Imagine feeling peaceful, joyful and content on a daily basis. It's the place to achieve greatness from. Practice "Radical Self Love" and watch miracles happen in your life.

Knowing yourself, your values and strengths is the fourth concept that enables you to cultivate a powerful mind. I want you to take a practical approach to this one. There are assessments, evaluations and tests out there that can give you valuable insights into how you can be more effective and successful.

To help my clients get to know themselves better fast I love to use the Values Index (http://en.wikipedia.org/wiki/Eduard_Spranger) and the DISC assessment (http://en.wikipedia.org/wiki/DISC_assessment). The results help them understand how they tend to approach things, and what the best conditions for them are to shine in both their personal and professional lives. It is also extremely powerful for me, as a coach, to know how my clients are "wired." The assessments eliminate frustrating questions like: "Why do I always do that?" and "Why can't I just be more like this." My clients can see where they need to make changes and finally establish conditions conducive to their success.

I remember the day I got a call from my team leader, congratulating me on my first "$9000 month." More were sure to come. While he talked I thought: "Oh well, I'll pay this bill and that bill and so what?" I wasn't feeling happy or excited. This in turn caused me to question my motives: "Isn't this what you wanted? Can't you ever have enough? What does it take to make you happy?" Oh, how great we are at being our own worst enemy! I would never talk to my friends this way! The truth was that I was not living according to my core values, rendering me miserable. Luckily, I found out about this concept shortly after the call. It is unbelievable how blind I was to this concept until I was made aware of it. As I discovered my core values and took a look at my life and career, everything suddenly made sense. While I was making money, which was not a core value of mine, I didn't feel as though I was contributing to the world or connecting with enough human beings. Instead, I was spending six hours a day in my car, speaking only for an hour or so with potential clients in the financial industry. With connection and contribution being my top two values, it was no wonder I felt depressed. In fact, it was then that I decided to change careers and follow my passion. It is where I gained the confidence to dedicate my life to being a coach and inspiring others to upgrade their lives and follow their own passions. Today, I constantly ask myself: "Does this action/thing I'm about to do align with my values?" If it doesn't, I move on.

In school, we are usually taught to focus on the subjects we aren't so good at. If we're not good at math, we're supposed to do more of it. If we're sorry spellers, more reading and writing is called for. While I absolutely agree that it is necessary to have certain knowledge and skill base, teaching kids to focus on what they aren't good at, is quite possibly diminishing their chance of discovering just how magnificent they could be at something they are now good at.

Focus your attention on the things you are good at and check if you can outsource some of those things you clearly weren't born to do. Are you great at connecting with people, but cleaning your house is a pain? Clearly, a housekeeper can make your home shine while you are out creating opportunity for business through networking. Is making money easy for you, but you never seem to be able to hold on to it? Hire an accountant, CPA or financial consultant instead of trying to become an expert in investing yourself. It's a simple concept, yet due to our conditioning we often spend too much time trying to get better at things that aren't our inherent strengths, and not nearly enough time perfecting the skills we already have great aptitude for.

When I took the Strengths Test (http://www.strengthstest.com) I noticed that each of my top 10 strengths ended with "for others." At first I thought: "So I can't do anything for myself? That's not good." Then it hit me: Being a coach, isn't it absolutely wonderful that I have an inherent ability to look at someone else's situation and give valuable insights to help them make positive changes in their life? I'd just have to figure out a way to outsource all the other important parts of my business and focus on being with my clients. This was exciting news!

Can you see how implementing the four concepts I just described will enable you to take charge of your thoughts in a way that doesn't require willpower but instead creates a powerful mind with which you can accomplish greatness? By feeding your positive thought, reclaiming your story, practicing radical self-love and getting to know yourself, your values and strengths, you can establish the perfect conditions for personal growth and lasting positive changes in your life. As I promised you at the beginning, you can begin to implement most of these concepts right away. Now it's your turn!

To Contact Sonja-Sophie

Claim your free gift at www.SonjaSophie.com

coachsonjasophie@gmail.com

Call 323-873-6442 Promo Code CHANGE to receive a special price on a DISC and Values Assessment Debriefing Session with her now.

Glenda Fleming-Thomas

Glenda Fleming-Thomas is the owner of integrated Life Coaching. She has been helping people on their healing journeys for over 25 years. She works custom programs for people who are ready to go from the quicksand to the best quality of life ever!

She is an inspirational speaker, who presents workshops and joint venture tele-seminars and more. Glenda is an author and online radio show host.

Contemplating Change

By Glenda Fleming –Thomas

Are you familiar with any of these quotes?

"Be the change you wish to see in the world," - Gandhi

"Things change. And friends leave. Life doesn't stop for anybody." - Stephen Chbosky

"Everyone thinks of changing the world but no one thinks of changing himself." - Leo Tolstoy

"Never doubt that a small group of thoughtful, committed, citizens can change the world. Indeed, it is the only thing that ever has." - Margaret Mead

"Education is the most powerful weapon which you can use to change the world." - Nelson Mandela

"The world as we have created it is a process of our thinking. It cannot be changed without changing our thinking." - Albert Einstein

"Change will not come if we wait for some other people, or if we wait for some other time. We are the ones we've been waiting for. We are the changes that we seek." - Barack Obama

"And that is how change happens. One gesture. One person. One moment at a time." - Libba Bray

"Stepping onto a brand-new path is difficult, but not more difficult than remaining in a situation, which is not nurturing to the whole woman." - Maya Angelou

CHANGE is something that every human being on the face of the earth has in common. Change happens to us, around us and even in us, whether we want it to or not. How we choose to deal with change differs. What we choose to change differs. Why we change differs. When we change differs. Who accepts change differs. Where change takes place differs. One thing that is constant however, is CHANGE.

As we contemplate change, first I wish to define what "contemplation" is and is not. Contemplation is not a quick, aimless glance, according to the Encarta Dictionary (North America). The primary definition of contemplate is "to think about something as a possible course of action." The secondary meaning is "to think about something seriously and at length, especially in order to understand it more fully." The tertiary meaning is "to think calmly and at length, especially as a religious or spiritual exercise." Finally, the fourth level definition is "to look at something thoughtfully and steadily." Though unusual and unexpected, I include all four definitions of contemplation in this writing.

The Nature of CHANGE:

1. Change is constant. Change is all over the place! Every human being and every living thing on earth experiences CHANGE.

- Change of life.
- Change of seasons.

- Change of heart.

- Changing diapers.

- Change in the weather.

- Changing the channels.

Change is all around us!

2. Your resistance is futile. We may resist change in others, in ourselves and even the world around us, but we still end up changing in some other area or being changed in a more unexpected passive way. Why resist when you can choose to change?

3. CHANGE is neutral. Change is neither good nor bad. Our beliefs about CHANGE determine how we respond to it. For example, if I believe that making a move from this city is bad or if I believe that moving from this city is good, I am right either way. What we believe about people, places and things directly impacts how well we adapt to the change. If we tell ourselves it is bad, our experience tends to live down to that belief. Change is unbiased. Change just is.

MY 1st MILESTONE

My first milestone of personal development was when I decided to see a psychotherapist.

What precipitated this decision was a myriad of physical problems. These problems were persistent and I continued to have to go into the emergency room to get help. Some of my symptoms were panic attacks, migraine headaches, agoraphobia, general anxiety and depression.

In the middle 1980s, I recognized that I had agoraphobia. When I was in public places like church or at a professional basketball games in large arenas, or when I was in large crowds, I felt very nervous and dizzy.

My first major crisis was after we made a move. In 1979, we moved from Tacoma, Washington, to Denver, Colorado, where my husband J C Thomas, Jr., was the minister. A young mother of 3, I did not know anyone there and I missed the people we left behind. Everything came to a head one night: I was lying in bed with my husband and my body began shaking uncontrollably. I woke him up and I told him to take me to the hospital. Once the doctor examined me and asked me about my stress level, he explained that I had been pushing down my feelings of missing people that I left behind. I was forcing myself to not cry and to not feel my feelings. My feelings came through my body, revealing to me I needed to pay attention to my emotions. He gave me instructions on how to allow myself to feel my feelings and to cry when I felt like it. The doctor explained that my emotions were not being released, so my body let me know there was something I needed to pay attention to. This was the first time I learned and experienced how the mind and the body are intricately connected.

In 1983, we moved from Colorado to California, in between churches again. We lived at my parents for a while before my husband started working at another church. (By this time we had 3 children.) My panic attacks had escalated from agoraphobia. When I went to do my grocery shopping was when I noticed the panic attacks most. The episode would be this inner turmoil and struggle of trying to stay in the store and finish my shopping, when all I felt like doing was running out screaming. My heart was pounding hard and my pulse was racing. I was feeling out of breath and I had racing thoughts. I questioned myself as to whether I should stay in the store and finish shopping or if I should leave. Then I started thinking to myself, "I have got to get out of here!" My thoughts would dart to the consequences if I left there. I'd have to start all over again and my family would not have any food to eat. This happened for months and months. Then one day I was looking at the television, (I believe it was the Oprah Winfrey Show), I heard her guests talking about panic attacks and what they felt like. As they started to describe how they were feeling, I realized that that's exactly what I was going through and I had no idea that there was a name for it until then - panic attacks.

We began working at another church and after that, I began to experience more frequent panic attacks - and they were much more intense. I would periodically call 911 to be taken to the emergency room. One day I was feeling really, really bad. My heart was pounding, the typical frightening pace. I experienced everything that went along with the panic attack. I told my husband to take me over to San Francisco to the UCSF hospital. I wanted to go right then, while I still had the symptoms. I wanted to see if they could discover if I was having a heart attack or something. I had been through this so many times! The symptoms would be so bad, I felt like I was going to die and I really thought I was. J C drove me to the doctor and this was the day that everything came to a head. He gave me the typical examination to check my new nervous system to make sure I wasn't having a stroke or a heart attack.

The doctor came in and he said these words that mortified me, "Mrs. Thomas, I'm not saying that you are crazy, but there is nothing wrong with you." He told me that I needed to go to my Community Health Clinic and tell them that I needed to see a doctor and then they could refer me to a therapist. At this point, I knew that my distress was beyond physical and apparently was something psychological. So I began to pray because I did not have any money to pay for a therapist. I did not know how the Community Health Clinic would work for me. It turned out that because of the income level and the number of people that were in our family, I didn't have to

The Change 3

pay for the psychotherapist. I had some hesitancy about getting into therapy because, of course, I had never done it before.

Deep down inside in my spirit, I knew that I had suffered enough and I was sick and tired of being sick and tired. Besides all these things going on, I was also suffering from depression periodically - and I was functional but I was miserable. I walked around feeling like there was a hole in my gut. At other times I literally felt the weight of the world on my shoulders. I absolutely didn't know what else to do. I prayed for God's guidance and I went to the doctor at the Community Health Clinic in Richmond. He recommended me to the therapist who worked there and thus began my journey with psychotherapy. She was a licensed clinical social worker.

Along with therapy, I read success books. I listened to affirmations on audio tapes. I decided to use tapes to help re-program my subconscious mind with positive thoughts and a loving attitude for myself. I allowed the process to happen.

Over a span of about three years and several months, I worked with this psychotherapist and things changed. What changed? My sense of self was stronger. I did not feel that hole in the center of my body. I felt well! I felt healed. I could see the sunshine instead of the gray skies. My self-esteem was higher. I learned to replace the repetitive disapproving voice recording telling me, "You shouldn't feel that way." I learned to replace those words with loving and respectful encouragement. I began to allow myself to feel my feelings and allow my feelings to be. I was able to speak up for myself more consistently. I was ready to work on my spiritual growth.

A while after I completed therapy and ended my sessions, a woman came into my life and introduced me to the 12 steps for Christians. I had been given the book by someone maybe a year before, but I never looked at it or knew what it was about. When the time was right, this person came into my life and helped me work up to Step

4. When the time was right, she left the process and then I worked the rest of The Steps on my own. This spiritual awakening was a huge life changer. I began to understand the difference between spiritual awakening versus "going to church." I went to church all my life. My husband was a minister and I was a minister's wife and teacher and leader in my own right. Now I began to understand my relationship with Spirit and the psychological, and how they are linked to one another. Therefore, I could no longer isolate the spiritual from the psychological or from the physical. My mental issues were what caused me to have physical problems, which led to psychological issues, which led to seek my spiritual awakening. So they are all tied together - body, mind and spirit - they are all integrated. And today, that's why I call the kind of coaching I do, "Integrated Life Coaching."

MY 2nd MILESTONE

I began reading personal development or self-improvement materials in 1977 or 1978. My primary interest was learning about self-esteem - what it was and how to improve my self-esteem. In 1987 maybe, I began to realize that just reading about self-improvement was not enough. I really wanted to live a higher quality of life - like I read about and witnessed other people seeming to live. I knew I wanted to change. I needed to change.

I decided to test out some of the things I have been reading about. One thing I read about was that the energy that we put out into the world shows up in our lives. And that we are 100% responsible for what shows up in our lives.

So I decided to change my negative thoughts and replace them with affirmations.

Here are some of the negative thoughts that I needed to replace: "No one listens to me." "I am not interesting." "People don't care about what I think." I determined that I would replace those thoughts with, "People want to hear what I have to say." "I am a very interesting person," and "People care about what I think."

My plan was to simply change my thoughts. I did not tell anyone anything about my experiment. So I went about silently and watched the results. For a day, then weeks, I became an observer in my life lab. I was beginning a lifestyle of being self-observant. I noticed that people did listen to me. Some leaned in when I spoke. An encouraging person came into my life. People responded in positive ways to what I shared in public speaking or in private. My world changed.

My 3rd Milestone

My 3rd milestone began six months ago from this November, 2014. I started in June. A business coach found me on LinkedIn and said that she was offering free strategy sessions. I decided to see what this was all about. She was offering strategy sessions to help build my business. This was a different kind of experience for me because it was a group of women and included one on one coaching with the program as well. I decided to participate in this group which lasted six months. The program was set up so that we had conference calls every other week with the group, and then every other week in between. The coach interacted with us on our specific strategies as they related to the concepts we talked about on the conference call with the group.

Being involved with this group and this business coach helped me overcome issues that were hindering my business:

    Fear of stepping out.

    Fear of letting my light shine.

    Not clear about what I do to help people.

Uncomfortable with charging proper fees reflecting my value.

Feeling a lack of support.

As a result of our six months together, I stepped out and designed and hosted an event. I overcame the fear of hosting this event. I had been stuck in that fear because of the painful acts of others. I finally stepped up and did it. The event went excellently. I overcame the fear of letting my light shine. I began to really believe and understand that my deep desire to positively impact lives is important. We had in-depth conversations. I learned through activities and through listening to the stories of the other women in the group. I learned how important it was that I show up. I became convinced that there are people waiting for me to show up. I changed from being unclear about what I do and I became clear about what I do and how my coaching, teaching and life blesses others. I discovered why my work is so valuable. I changed. Now I am comfortable with charging proper fees. I accepted the support of the women in the group. They wanted me to be successful. We all wanted each another to be successful. The coach wanted me to be successful and it was all genuine! The connectedness between us was a real. I changed. I now have tools to face my challenges and to help others.

My 4th Milestone

Near the end of the group coaching, I received an email from Jim Britt through LinkedIn. We had a conversation along with Jim Lutes regarding co-authoring this book, "The Change." I contemplated all the things I had learned in conjunction with my life experiences and my desire to go to another level. I knew that this would be an awesome opportunity for me to be a part of this book. This was my Big Break! So I said, "Yes." I had no earthly idea how I would keep my commitment but what I did know was that I wanted to be a part of this book. The resources I needed showed up at the perfect time for me to be a part of this book "The Change: Book 3."

Concluding Contemplations

My life has been an interesting journey .There have been ups and downs and moments of confusion and years of pain and suffering. I have come through all of these different hills and valleys to get to where I am today. I am experiencing the connectedness of body, mind and spirit.

How did CHANGE happen for me?

It was fast, it was slow. It was easy and it was difficult. Change was what I looked forward to and it was what I dreaded the most. CHANGE is multifaceted. Since I have a choice, I choose to go with the flow of each phase of my life. I choose to surrender myself to be CHANGED. I choose to GROW. What's ahead? A new adventure!

To all who read this book, I send you love and respect for your journey.

I will walk with you on your journey to a brighter, freer, accomplished life. I work with coachable individuals who are feeling stuck and are fully ready to move from the quicksand to the highest quality life ever! I offer a premium 6 month and 1 year package to go from the quicksand to the highest quality life ever!

Connect with me at:

coachglenda7@gmail.com

http://glendathomas.wordpress.com

Contemplating Change

http://livingoutpersonalvalues.wordpress.com

Twitter@coachglenda7

AFTERWORD

Life is always a series of transitions… people, places and things that shape who we are as individuals. Often, you never know that the next catalyst for change is around the corner.

Jim Britt and Jim Lutes have spent decades influencing individuals to blossom into the best version of themselves.

Allow all you have read in this book to create introspection and redirection if required. It's your journey to craft.

The Change is a series. A global movement. Watch for future releases and add them to your collection. If you know of anyone who would like to be considered as a co-author for a future book, have them email our offices at support@jimbritt.com.

The individual and combined works of Jim Britt and Jim Lutes have filled seminar rooms to maximum capacity and created a worldwide demand.

The blessings go both ways as Jim and Jim are always willing students of life. Out of demand for life changing programs and events, Jim and Jim conduct seminars worldwide as well as created a global company in over 170 countries called Quanta International that allows anyone to benefit behaviorally as well as financially.

Contemplating Change

If you would like to hear more about how the Quanta company can assist you in both income generating and personal development, please email our offices at: quanta@jimbritt.com.

To Schedule Jim Britt or Jim Lutes as your featured speaker at your next convention or special event, email: support@jimbritt.com.

Master your moment as they become hours that become days.

Your legacy awaits.

Blessings,

Jim Britt and Jim Lutes

www.ingramcontent.com/pod-product-compliance
Lightning Source LLC
Chambersburg PA
CBHW071900290426
44110CB00013B/1224